Cambridge Elements ≡

Elements in the Philosophy of Mathematics
edited by
Penelope Rush
University of Tasmania
Stewart Shapiro
The Ohio State University

MATHEMATICS IS (MOSTLY) ANALYTIC

Gregory Lavers
Concordia University

CAMBRIDGE
UNIVERSITY PRESS

Shaftesbury Road, Cambridge CB2 8EA, United Kingdom

One Liberty Plaza, 20th Floor, New York, NY 10006, USA

477 Williamstown Road, Port Melbourne, VIC 3207, Australia

314–321, 3rd Floor, Plot 3, Splendor Forum, Jasola District Centre,
New Delhi – 110025, India

103 Penang Road, #05–06/07, Visioncrest Commercial, Singapore 238467

Cambridge University Press is part of Cambridge University Press & Assessment,
a department of the University of Cambridge.

We share the University's mission to contribute to society through the pursuit of
education, learning and research at the highest international levels of excellence.

www.cambridge.org
Information on this title: www.cambridge.org/9781009507363

DOI: 10.1017/9781009109925

First published 2024

A catalogue record for this publication is available from the British Library.

ISBN 978-1-009-50736-3 Hardback
ISBN 978-1-009-11111-9 Paperback
ISSN 2399-2883 (online)
ISSN 2514-3808 (print)

Cambridge University Press & Assessment has no responsibility for the persistence
or accuracy of URLs for external or third-party internet websites referred to in this
publication and does not guarantee that any content on such websites is, or will
remain, accurate or appropriate.

Mathematics is (mostly) Analytic

Elements in the Philosophy of Mathematics

DOI: 10.1017/9781009109925
First published online: December 2024

Gregory Lavers
Concordia University

Author for correspondence: Gregory Lavers, greg.lavers@Concordia.ca

Abstract: This Element outlines and defends an account of analyticity according to which mathematics is, for the most part, analytic. The author begins by looking at Quine's arguments against the concepts of analyticity. He shows how Quine's position on analyticity is related to his view on explication and shows how this suggests a way of defining analyticity that would meet Quine's own standards for explication. The author then looks at Boghossian and his distinction between epistemic and metaphysical accounts of analyticity. Here he argues that there is a straightforward way of eliminating the confusion Boghossian sees with what he calls metaphysical accounts. The author demonstrates that the epistemic dimension of his epistemic account is almost entirely superfluous. The author then discusses how analyticity is related to truth, necessity, and questions of ontology. Finally, he discusses the vagueness of analyticity and also the relation of analyticity to the axiomatic method in mathematics.

Keywords: analyticity, Quine, Carnap, explication, mathematical truth

ISBNs: 9781009507363 (HB), 9781009111119 (PB), 9781009109925 (OC)
ISSNs: 2399-2883 (online), 2514-3808 (print)

Contents

1 Introduction

> There are also two kinds of truths, those of reasoning and those of fact. The truths of reasoning are necessary and their opposite is impossible; the truths of fact are contingent, and their opposite is possible. When a truth is necessary, its reason can be found by analysis, resolving it into simpler ideas and simpler truths until we reach the primitives. [Monadology 33][1]

There is quite a lot going on in this quote, although this quote from Leibniz is one of many in the history of philosophy expressing very much the same thought. Of course, we see, in this quote, a division of truths into two kinds, but we also see links with necessity and a connection with the process of analysis. Just after this, Leibniz goes on to explicitly include mathematics among the truths of reason. "This is how the speculative theorems and practical canons of mathematicians are reduced by analysis to definitions, axioms and postulates" (Ariew & Garber, 1989, Monadology 34). We see that truths of reason, including mathematics, are arrived at in a process of analysis, and thereby acquire the property of being necessary and knowable by means of logic (together with the aforementioned analysis).

In the early twentieth century something very close to this picture was still widely held. However, this view fell out of favor for two reasons in the second half of the twentieth century. First, of course, there was, following Quine's "Two Dogmas of Empiricism," a widespread view that the notion of analyticity is suspect.[2] Analyticity, at the time, was the leading means for explaining how we could have knowledge by reason alone. But, whereas, for some time after the publication of "Two Dogmas …," the matter was seen by many to be settled in Quine's favor, there are now more and more philosophers and scientists looking once again at the concept of analyticity.[3] In fact, Chomsky, in a relatively recent work, writes:

---

[1] This translation is from Ariew and Garber (1989).

[2] That said, in recent surveys of philosophers, discussed in Bourget and Chalmers (2023), in both the 2009 and 2020 surveys about 65% of philosophers agreed that there is an analytic/synthetic distinction. This while only 27% in 2009 and 21% in 2020 rejecting the distinction (with 8% and 16% respectively answering "other"). This means that philosophers are about three times as likely to accept vs. reject this distinction, despite the attacks from Quine and others.

[3] A recent example of a defense of the concept is given in Russell (2008). Russell wishes to reject the dilemma that either a sentence is made true entirely by the meaning of the terms involved or it is made true at least in part by the world. Quine argued that every true sentence is in part true in virtue of what it means, and in part because of how the world is. Russell wishes to allow that even if an analytic claim is true, in a sense, because of how the world is, it can nonetheless *completely determined* by the meaning of the terms involved. The world only redundantly determines the truth of the claim.

I take a different tact in addressing these arguments expressing doubts about how it can be that the meaning of a term can make some claim true. This is discussed in Section 3.

> If the best argument for dispensing with the analytic–synthetic distinction
> is that it is of no use to the field linguist, then virtually everyone who actu-
> ally works in descriptive semantics, or ever has, must be seriously in error,
> since such work is shot through with assumptions about connections of
> meaning, which will (in particular) induce examples of the analytic-synthetic
> distinction. (Chomsky, 2000, p. 47)[4]

Crispin Wright once remarked in the opening paragraphs of one of his papers, "I myself do not believe that when the dust settles on analytical philosophy's first century, our successors will find that the notion of analyticity was discredited by any of the well-known assaults"(Wright, 2001, p. 7). One of the things I will attempt in this work is to contribute to settling this very dust.

The second major reason the view discussed in the Leibniz quote earlier is now widely abandoned is that it assumes the coextension of these truths of reason with what is necessary. Since the later half of the twentieth century the view that analyticity, necessity, and *a priority* all coincide has fallen out of favor. I am not here advocating a return to mid twentieth-century philosophy of mathematics. I will not at all try to argue against the now almost universally acknowledged view that the concepts of necessary truths, analytic truths, and a priori truths do not all coincide.

The present work, although, historically informed, is not principally a work in the history of philosophy. I want to formulate a natural definition of *analyticity* such that it includes, at least most of mathematics, and such that it can be defended against well-known arguments. As Quine's arguments are usually seen as the greatest obstacle to an account of analyticity, I do want to show that Quine's argument against the possibility of successfully explicating *analyticity* can be answered, and that the account given is such a successful explication by Quine's own standards. As a result, Section 2 will involve more attention to historical positions than the other sections.

The term *analytic*, of course, comes from Kant. "Either the predicate B belongs to the subject A as something that is (covertly) contained in this con-cept A; or B lies entirely outside the concept A, though to be sure it stands in connection with it. In the first case I call the judgment analytic, in the second synthetic" (Guyer & Wood, 1998, A6 B10). Kant describes analytic truth as non-ampliative. Kant does not include mathematics among the analytic truths for this reason: mathematical proofs *are* ampliative. They depend for him on

---

[4] The account of analytic truth put forward and defended in this Element is not as empirically motivated as what Chomsky seems to have in mind here. I do not wish to claim that the account defended here is the only reasonable way of making the analytic/synthetic distinction, just that it is a particularly useful one for use in philosophy, including philosophy of mathematics and philosophy of science more generally.

our pure intuitions of space and time. Frege, contrary to this Kantian view, attempts to show that, except in the case of geometry, all mathematical concepts are definable on the basis of pure logic, and that mathematical theorems are derivable by purely logical means from these definitions. As is well known, Frege's attempt to carry out this project in detail in his *Grundgesetze der Arithmetik* turned out to be inconsistent. This is because of his Basic Law V which leads to Russell's Paradox. One might think that to overcome this problem one could formulate a Fregean view in a consistent background theory. However, the prospects for this project *or anything like it* was called into question by Gödel's First Incompleteness Theorem. No longer could the notion of mathematical truth, so far as it is expressible in a formal system, be reduced to formal derivability. A reduction of mathematics to logic seemed impossible.

Carnap's reaction to this situation, in his *The Logical Syntax of Language* (*Syntax*) of 1934, is to define a notion of consequence stronger than derivability. This is done for, for instance, by adding infinitary rules of inference (like an ω-rule). In this way, although not all mathematical truths expressible in the language are derivable, they are still *consequences* of the empty set of sentences. All of mathematics is thus analytic on Carnap's view. Under the influence of Wittgenstein's notion of a tautology, Carnap defines the content of a sentence to be the set of it's non-analytic consequences. A mathematical truth is true however the world happens to be, because it says nothing about how the world happens to be. To say something about the world we must express ourselves with a descriptive claim (neither analytic nor contradictory). And so by definition an analytic claim is an empty claim which says nothing about the world.

Quine describes himself as a disciple of Carnap's for six years after the time of *Syntax*. Even after this period, he holds very much the same view as Carnap on the subject of the analyticity of mathematical truth up to, at least, 1947. In a paper from this year (Quine, 1947) he gives a definition of analyticity which includes all of the non-recursively enumerable set of mathematical truths. Quine's eventual rejection of analyticity does not stem from a problem he saw with Carnap's appeal to strong consequence relations for the definition of mathematical truth. It was when Carnap began to apply the concept of analyticity outside of the logico-mathematical context that Quine started to take issue. Quine also had a strong distrust of any kind of intensional notions. His plan, at this time, is to use synonymy to define analyticity. It was not until, after many years, Quine realizes that his project of defining synonymy in extensional terms (in fact, ultimately in behaviouristic terms) was proving completely fruitless, that he decides to reject the notion altogether. Quine devotes significant thought to this project between 1943 and 1949. To a great extent, "Two

Dogmas ..." is Quine's announcement that he has abandoned his own project of attempting to defining *synonymy* and *analyticity* in a manner that would meet his standards.

As mentioned, Quine's "Two Dogmas..." is largely seen as refuting Carnap's use of analyticity. In particular, it is seen as undermining Carnap's philosophy of mathematics. Now, Carnap's philosophy of mathematics, whether one agrees with it or not, must be recognized as having some very nice features. Because all analytic truths are mere tautologies which say nothing about the world, we are free to accept any set of them as stipulations. Since, we can accept any set of axioms and rules of inference (including infinitary rules of inference to define a strong consequence relation), all of mathematics can then be included in the analytic truths. As we are often able to determine what follows from these stipulations, there are no serious obstacles for an epistemology of mathematics. What is analytic, or logically true in the language system, is meant to capture the idea of what is true by necessity. Descriptive claims, if true, are true in virtue of contingent facts, but analytic truths are true independently of such claims. So this view also explains the apparent necessity of mathematics. Furthermore, as argued in Carnap (1950a), we can accept any language system we want and there is no special problem introduced when accepting a system of analytic sentences which make ontological demands. So when I say the view has nice features, I am referring to the fact that it purports to explain, all at once, so to speak, the epistemology, apparent necessity and ontological implications of mathematics. Also, given the role of *explication* in Carnap's philosophy, which will be dealt with in some detail in the next section, it also explains how mathematical claims are seen as conceptual truths.

While I have argued in the last paragraph that this view does have some nice features, there are several reasons why it is no longer accepted today. One sees that central to the Carnapian picture of the philosophy of mathematics just discussed is the concept of analyticity. So one reason it is not widely accepted today is that this notion is viewed by many with suspicion. There are at least two more problems that some may identify with the Carnapian view just discussed. One is the coextension of the analytic, the a priori, and the necessary. The other feature of the Carnapian view that many would take issue with is his use of Wittgenstein's idea of a tautology.[5]

In the present work I do not intend to defend a Carnapian picture of the analyticity of mathematics, but I do wish to defend the view that mathematics is (for the most part) analytic. What I want to do is argue that there is a clear way

---

[5] Of course, Wittgenstein himself did not take mathematical statements to be tautologies.

to define *analytic* such that it will contain, if not all, the vast majority of mathematics. In fact, this definition will be based on a distinction that Quine himself discusses and uses. What I will not do is argue that this coincides with the a priori or with necessary truth. Nor will I be defending the position that mathematics is tautological in Wittgenstein's sense. So while I praised earlier the extensiveness of Carnap's philosophy of mathematics, in terms of explaining, in one stroke, the necessity, the *a priority*, the ontology, and even conceptual nature of mathematics, the project of this Element is far more narrow. I take it that identifying what I believe to be an interesting and natural way to define analyticity, and to argue that this includes most of mathematics, will be an important step toward understanding the nature of mathematical truth.

One of my goals will be to remove something of a taboo, caused by attacks on *analyticity*, on the, until recently, widely held view that mathematical truths are conceptual truths. Perhaps the value of the argument that mathematics is (mostly) analytic, in the sense described here, cannot fully be appreciated until a fuller account of the epistemology of mathematics can be worked out. That is beyond the scope of what is possible in this short Element, but what is shown here is an important step in that direction. The account of analyticity given, although it will distance this concept from the concepts of necessity and *a priority*, will, nonetheless, be closely linked with the notion of a conceptual truth. There is obviously a story to be told about the relation between the epistemology of mathematics and the view that mathematical truths are conceptual truths. As mentioned I will not defend any epistemological position but merely point out that the view, that mathematical truths are conceptual truths, arrived at by a process of analysis of our concepts, was held by both Gödel and Carnap (details in Section 4). So the position defended in this Element is compatible with a range of epistemological positions. Also, while I am not defending a Carnapian philosophy of mathematics generally, I do defend a position on the ontological demands of our conceptual schemes (also in Section 4) which resembles to a fair extent the position of Carnap (1950a).

In the next section I will look at Quine's arguments against the concept of analyticity. I argue that both Carnap and Quine see the dispute over analyticity as a challenge of coming up with an *explication* of the concept. The term *explication* Quine takes from Carnap, but Quine understands the constraints on explications differently from Carnap.[6] Their different views on explication, end up, on my analysis, being responsible for their different pronouncements on the subject of the definability of a notion of analyticity. I take it that following

---

[6] I argue this as well in Lavers (2012), but the argument here is considerably extended, and defended in light of some responses.

from this discussion, a natural definition of analyticity, which satisfies Quine's demands of an explication, suggests itself. I then look at the relation between the suggested definition of analyticity and what Quine says regarding the status of arithmetic and set theory.

Another famous critique of the traditional concept of analyticity is given in Paul Boghossian's (Boghossian, 1996). This will be the principal focus of Section 3. Boghossian does not want to reject analyticity altogether. What he rejects is what he calls a *metaphysical conception* of analyticity. In its place he suggests an *epistemic* concept of analyticity. The view I explain, motivate, and defend in Section 2 is not an epistemic conception of analyticity, so it may be thought that Boghossian's arguments count against the concept which I define. I argue that once a particular confusion is cleared up, there is no problem with the so-called *metaphysical* conception (or at least with a non-epistemic notion). Furthermore, I argue that Boghossian's epistemic conception is, in essence, the *same* conception, and so not *essentially epistemic*, but then turned into an epistemic theory via some dubious epistemic assumptions.

As mentioned, the account of analyticity I defend is not meant to be coextensive with either the a priori or with necessary truth. It is also not meant to be motivated by Wittgenstein's account of tautologies as saying nothing of the world. The account of analyticity I put forward is meant to capture conceptual truths and to be distinct from what might be true by (arbitrary) stipulation. Section 4 will look at how the account of analyticity put forward relates to other concepts just mentioned. I will also discuss here the relation of analyticity to the ordinary notion of truth. Lastly I will make some comments about how to understand the ontological demands of mathematics.

In the final section, I look quickly at a couple more potential problems for the suggested account. The first problem is the problem of vagueness. While many everyday concepts are vague in many ways that would impede our identification of what is analytic of them, this problem does not arise to anywhere near the same degree when we are considering mathematical concepts. I conclude by discussing the relation between the account of analyticity put forward and defended in this Element with the axiomatic method in mathematics.

2 Quine and Analyticity

Most who would deny the analyticity of mathematics would likely point to Quinean reasons for this. It is then important to look closely at Quine on analyticity and mathematics. To understand Quine's position on the analyticity of mathematics, we need to understand the Carnapian view of mathematical truth, which Quine wishes to preserve for a long time before ultimately rejecting. It might be thought that Quine, from quite early on, wants to do away with the concept of analyticity. It may also be thought that Quine, long before 1950, is skeptical of the use Carnap wanted to make of analyticity in his epistemology of mathematics and the sciences. While it is true that Quine rejects Carnap's specific definition of analyticity in the early 1940s, even in 1949 Quine is still attempting to preserve a broadly Carnapian philosophy of mathematics.[7] Until 1949, while Quine rejects modal logic and is skeptical of intensional notions generally, he thinks it an important task to define analyticity and synonymy behavioristically. In fact, Quine, at the time, thinks it is foolhardy to do away with meaning and analyticity altogether. One of the main motivations for thinking it was important to define analyticity was the preservation of a broadly Carnapian philosophy of mathematics. So let us begin by looking at the Carnapian position which was influential on the early Quine.

In *Syntax*, Carnap heeds the lesson of Gödel's First Incompleteness Theorem, but still wishes to defend some form of logicism. Much of the book consists of outlining and investigating the logical properties of two logical systems, which he calls *Language I* and *Language II*. For both his Language I and II, in response to Gödel's results, Carnap defines notions of *consequence* which are stronger than *deducibility*, and are, in fact, not recursively enumerable. For Language I, consequence is defined via an ω-rule. That is to say, if for every numeral "n" the sentence "$P(n)$" is *derivable* from a set of sentences, then the sentence "$\forall x P(x)$" is a *consequence* of those sentences. Thus we get a notion of consequence stronger than derivability. The Gödel sentence for Language I – a universal claim whose instances are all provable, so long as Language I is consistent – will then not be derivable from the primitive sentences (axioms) of Language I, but it is nonetheless a consequence of them, and thus analytic. For Language II, consequence is defined in terms of an intended interpretation of every type in the language. So while not every true mathematical claim, expressible in the language, can be deduced, it is nonetheless a consequence of the empty class of sentences and what Carnap calls *analytic*.

In 1934, Quine gives a series of lectures at Harvard on Carnap's views at the time of *Syntax*. Here Quine sees no problem defining analyticity and related notions:

> Then we can proceed in the same arithmetical fashion to the various derivative syntactic notions, such as "consequence," "analytic," "synthetic," "synonymity," "content," and so on; all of these, or rather the numbers

---

[7] See Verhaegh (2018) and Lavers (2022). Lavers (2022) deals with the role of Ruth Barcan Marcus's early work, most importantly Barcan (1946), in Quine's changing views on the subject of analyticity.

correlated with these, admit of purely arithmetical definition in terms of prime numbers and so on. The whole of syntax becomes, in effect, a branch of pure arithmetic. (Quine & Carnap, 1990, p. 84)

Of course, this is during Carnap's so-called syntactic phase. It was not until Carnap's semantic phase that Quine begins to express serious doubts regarding the concept of analyticity. But as Frost-Arnold has argued (Frost-Arnold, 2013), it was only when Carnap extends his definition of analyticity beyond logico-mathematical truths and into natural language that Quine begins to raise serious objections. Carnap's semantic definition of logico-mathematical truth in his encyclopedia article "Foundations of Mathematics" (Carnap, 1939/1955) did not raise Quine's suspicions. It was not until Carnap extends his definition of analyticity to include such ordinary sentences such as "All mares are horses" that Quine objects. For our purposes, it is important to observe that, at least initially, Quine's objections to Carnap's definitions of analyticity around 1940 are not connected to Carnap's use of the concept to define logico-mathematical truth as analytic.

Quine expresses his complete rejection of analyticity in "Two Dogmas ...." But when later, after accepting a limited role for analyticity, his position under-goes a reversal. We saw earlier that early on, he is happy to use the concept *analytic* for logico-mathematical truths, but is skeptical of Carnap's extension of this concepts to ordinary claims like "all mares are horses." But when Quine recognizes a limited role for analyticity later on, his position is the opposite (not with regard to first-order logic, but with regard to mathematical truth). He allows for the analyticity of first-order logic and some everyday cases, but does not take all of (or even very much of) mathematics to count as analytic:

The crude criterion in *Roots of Reference*, based on word learning, is no help; we don't in general know how we learned a word, nor what truths were learned in the process. Nor do we have any reason to expect uniformity in this regard from speaker to speaker, and there is no reason to care. Elementary logic and the bachelor example are clear enough cases, but there is no going on from there. (Quine, 1991, p. 271)

But the reason we can no longer count mathematical truths among the analytic truths has to do with the particular definition of *analytic* given in *Roots of Reference*. There he defines an analytic truth as one which everyone learns the truth of when learning the component words. This would include some very basic sentences, such as "there are seven days in a week" and perhaps "all mares are horses," but it would not include, Quine argues, much of mathematics. However, as Burgess points out in his Burgess (2004), through Quine's arguments with Charles Parsons (see, for example, Parsons 1995) it becomes clear that Quine *needs* something like analyticity to explain the *obviousness* of mathematics. A mathematical claim may be true (via holism) in virtue of the role it plays in our total scientific understanding of the world, but that does not explain its obviousness. Being confirmed along with our best scientific theories is *certainly not* why a typical mathematician accepts a mathematical claim. So, at least prima facie a definition which included mathematics and based on a distinction which Quine acknowledges as meaningful would be superior to the type of definitions of *analyticity* that Quine himself offers.

Carnap, once he formulates his conception of an explication (first present in Carnap 1945) describes his definitions of analyticity as an explication of the notion of a logical truth.[8] As mentioned, Quine, up until at least 1949, is still looking for a behavioristic explication of synonymy. With such an explication, he hopes to define analyticity in such a way as to include all of mathematics. As is well known, by 1950, when he first presents "Two Dogmas ...," Quine concludes that the prospects for such an explication are not encouraging, and that ultimately the concept ought to be rejected. The notion of explication plays a central role in both of their thinking on the question of analyticity, and ultimately, on their understanding of mathematical truth. In this section we will look at the relations between their views an explication, mathematical truth and analyticity. We will then see how this points to a way that Quine himself could answer the challenge he posed in "Two Dogmas ...." It will be shown that Quine uses a concept which could be used to answer his challenge. In fact, this concept is based on a distinction that Quine himself clearly takes to be of philosophical importance and central to his conception of a successful philosophical analysis.

2.1 Carnap and Quine on Explication

Quine describes himself as a disciple of Carnap's for six years, from 1932, when Quine met him in Prague, while Carnap was composing *Syntax*, until 1938. But even as late as Quine (1947), where Quine is principally concerned with attacking quantified modal logic, he shows that he sees it as unproblematic that Carnap uses of a strong notion of analyticity to define mathematical truth. There Quine says that analytic claims, in a non-modal system, can be defined as statements "[d]educible by the logic of truth-functions and quantification from true statements containing only logical signs"(Quine, 1947, p. 43). Importantly, Quine points out that, as per Gödel, the class of *true statements* containing only logical signs is not recursively enumerable. Notice that the appeal to Gödel's

---

[8] Carnap sometimes uses L-truth for the same notion.

first incompleteness theorem in this context only makes sense if Quine thinks that all of arithmetic is both analytic and composed of only logical vocabulary. In 1947 then, in this sense at least, Quine has not moved far from a Carnapian position on logico-mathematical truth.[9]

Carnap first presents his account of explication in Carnap (1945), but his most detailed account is contained in Carnap (1950b). Reading Langford (1942/1968) shortly after its publication, the presentation, there, of the *paradox of analysis* had an effect on how Carnap saw the process of philosophical analysis.[10] The paradox of analysis is the claim that all analyses must be either incorrect or uninformative. For instance, if one were to say "to be A is to be B" then this is either incorrect or uninformative. For if A and B have the same meaning the claim is uninformative, but if they have different meanings, then the claim is incorrect. Inspired by the paradox of analysis, Carnap believes the idea of analysis as arriving at something identical to the *explicandum* is to be rejected. If the goal is not to arrive at *the same thing*, then, after an analysis, we must be introducing a new concept (i.e. something different) – which he calls the *explicatum*. Carnap proposes four conditions on successful explication. The conditions are those of *similarity, simplicity, precision*, and *fruitfulness*. The only one of these conditions which has anything to do with the explicandum, and is not solely concerned with the explicatum, is the first one: the explicatum has to be similar to the explicandum.[11] How similar must it be? Carnap's answer is that the explicatum needs to be sufficiently similar that it could be used in the place of the explicandum. The exact statement of the requirement of similarity is "[t]he explicatum is to be similar to the explicandum in such a way that, in most cases in which the explicandum has so far been used, the explicatum can be used; however, close similarity is not required, and considerable differences are permitted" (Carnap, 1950b, p. 7). So Carnap's condition of similarity imposes the weakest possible condition (given that the explicatum is meant to replace the explicandum) on the link between the explicandum and explicatum. It is for this reason that Carnap thought Quine's challenge from "Two Dogmas ..." was so easy to answer. The challenge was to define a concept of analyticity that goes beyond logical truth to include statements like "all bachelors are unmarried." Carnap proposed that this could be done via meaning

---

9 As a reviewer helpfully pointed out, it should be mentioned that they are not similar in the sense that while Carnap accepted a strong consequence relation to define analyticity, Quine here, while characterizing the same set of sentences appeals to only a derivability in first-order logic as a consequence relation.

10 Langford is referenced, for instance, in Carnap (1950b).

11 In Carnap's actual practice of giving explications, the explicandum plays a larger role than is suggested by his official account of explication.

postulates. A logical truth follows from logic alone, but an analytic truth follows from the meaning postulates together with the laws of logic. So long as the meaning postulates are chosen in a reasonable manner, this will lead to a concept of analyticity that is extensionally similar to what is ordinarily considered analytic.

In an article I published on this subject (Lavers, 2012), I argued that Carnap and Quine's differing conception of explication explained their differences on analyticity. The difference I point to is that when Quine discusses explication, he speaks of identifying and preserving certain features of the already existing expression. Features outside of these "favored contexts" are labeled "don't-cares."[12] This preservation of the use of expressions in these "favored contexts" is completely absent from Carnap's view on explication.[13]

For Quine explication is a two-step process. This, we saw earlier, is also true of Carnap. But unlike Carnap, for Quine, in the first stage, we must identify some central aspect of the meaning of the explicandum that we wish to preserve. For Quine, this central feature is relative to our purposes and interests, but this does not diminish the importance of this first stage.[14] Those aspects of the use of the explicandum which are not part of this are labeled "don't-cares." The first stage for Quine is principally concerned with distinguishing as clearly as possible between the "favored contexts" and the "don't-cares." We then, in the second phase, come up with a clearly defined substitute which while agreeing with the explicandum on the "favored contexts" may differ in any possible way over the "don't-cares."

---

[12] Talk of "favored contexts" is from Quine (1951/1963) and talk of "don't-cares" is from Quine (1960). Although these two phrases are not used in the same work, I find it useful to have names for both sides of the distinction which Quine is drawing and will use them as such. Although Quine talks of what I call the *favored contexts/don't-cares* distinction often when he talks of explication, he has no consistent name for this distinction.

[13] Since this paper, there have been a couple of other papers trying to identify the difference between Carnap and Quine on explication (see Gustafsson, 2014; Raab, 2024). Gustafsson, in particular, is critical of my interpretation of Quine on explication. Additionally, when I presented on related subjects, such as Quine's views on set theory, my claim that Quine thinks of explication as involving the preservation of some aspect of the explicandum, has been called into question. Subsequently I will show that there is ample evidence that this interpretation of his views on explication is correct.

[14] Gustafsson's disagreement with my view is in part that I did not sufficiently emphasize the pragmatic aspect of Quine's view on explication. I did, in my original article quote Quine saying that the choice of what it is we wish to preserve about the explicandum is relative to our purpose and interests. But then Gustafsson goes on to say it follows that I am mistaken to claim, for Quine, an adequate explication must by identifying a feature of the explicandum which we wish to preserve. But, of course, it is not at all in conflict with Quine's pragmatism to claim that he requires of an explication that we begin by identifying an aspect of the explicandum which we wish to preserve.

Quine is explicit about how he views explication in a number of places, but most discussions of explication are very brief. He usually begins by citing his agreement with Carnap's views on explication, and then Quine lays out his own view of the matter. The agreement he expresses with Carnap's view is tied to them both rejecting the idea that the definiendum and the definiens ought to be synonymous. In an explication our goal is to introduce a newly defined notion. But beyond this agreement their views on the matter are quite different. The most detailed account is contained in *Word & Object*, but even the very brief discussions show that he is very consistent on the subject. There is roughly one page of "Two Dogmas ..." which deals with explication. Here Quine asks whether it is possible to give a Carnapian explication of synonymy or analyticity. Then he lays out the following as his account of how explication is supposed to work:

> Any word worth explicating has some contexts which, as wholes, are clear and precise enough to be useful; and *the purpose of explication is to preserve the usage of these favored contexts* while sharpening the usage of other contexts. In order that a given definition be usable for purposes of explication, therefore, what is required is not that the definiendum in its antecedent usage be synonymous with the definiens, but just that each of these favored contexts of the definiendum, taken as a whole in its antecedent usage, be synonymous with the corresponding context of the definiens.[15] (Quine, 1951/1963, p. 25, my emphasis)

Here we see Quine, in his discussion of explication is putting forward a view exactly in line with the interpretation given earlier. The definiens and definiendum need not be everywhere synonymous, but must agree in the "favored contexts." He continues:

> Two alternative definientia may be equally appropriate for the purposes of a given task of explication and yet not be synonymous with each other; for they may serve interchangeably within the favored contexts but diverge elsewhere. (Quine, 1951/1963, p. 25)

Again we see that there are favored contexts in which the ordinary notion and any newly defined ones are meant to agree. Outside of these contexts, there can be differences between two acceptable explications.

---

[15] There is also a point made here that even explication involves intensional notions that he wishes to eliminate. It is not enough for the definiens and definiendum to agree in the favored contexts, they must be *synonymous* (i.e. necessarily agreeing). He presents this here as an insurmountable problem for giving an explication of analyticity. However, elsewhere he does not complain about this intensional aspect to explications and goes on to use the concept of an explication for years.

Quine's most detailed account of explication, as mentioned, is given in *Word & Object* (§53), it is exactly in line with the view already briefly discussed in "Two Dogmas ...." This section is given the title "The ordered pair as a philosophical paradigm." The reason given for the claim made in the title is that we can identify exactly what any analysis of ordered pair ought to preserve. What any account of the ordered pair must preserve is that $\langle x, y \rangle = \langle w, z \rangle$ only if $x = w$ and $y = z$. Quine sees the various definitions of the ordered pair as exemplars of philosophical analysis, because here it is so easy to identify the features of the ordinary notion that we wish to preserve. The various definitions are mutually inconsistent; if $\langle x, y \rangle = \{\{x\}, \{x, y\}\}$ then it is not, in general, identical with $\{\{x\}, \{y, \emptyset\}\}$. That is, the Kuratowski and Wiener definitions of the ordered pairs are competing accounts, but they are both successful analyses. Because each preserves the central feature of ordered pairs. Where they disagree is over what Quine terms "don't-cares." It is true that in this same section he says that this example is atypical of explication. "Our example is atypical in just one respect: the demands of partial agreement are preternaturally succinct and explicit" (Quine, 1960, §53) But notice the *one respect* in which this is atypical, is that in this case the "don't-cares" can be separated from what we wish to preserve with an incredibly simple to state principle. Other than this, this is a very typical explication.

Quine is well known to have said (again in *Word & Object* §53) that explication is elimination. This has led some to think that Quine saw explication as *ontological* elimination, but while this is sometimes true, explication does not always involve ontological elimination. Notice the conditional nature of this quote: "If there was a question of objects, and the partial parallelism which we are now picturing obtains, the corresponding objects of the new scheme will tend to be looked upon as the old mysterious objects minus the mystery" (Quine, 1960, §53). But importantly, Quine mentions Turing's analysis of a computable function as a paradigm of explication, and here, there is no ontological elimination, but rather a conceptual clarification. So while explication *can* lead to ontological elimination, it is always the elimination of an old defective term in favor of a more clearly defined one.

Let us return now to showing that Quine sees explication as involving the preservation of some feature of the use of the antecedent expression. Consider now this discussion of explication from *Word & Object*:

> This construction is paradigmatic of what we are most typically up to when in a philosophical spirit we offer an "analysis" or "explication" of some hitherto inadequately formulated "idea" or expression. We do not claim synonymy. We do not claim to make clear and explicit what users of the language had in

mind all along. We do not expose hidden meanings, as the words "analysis" and "explication" would suggest; we supply lacks. *We fix on the particular functions of the unclear expression that make it worth troubling about, and then devise a substitute, clear and couched in terms of our liking, that fills those functions.* Beyond those conditions of partial agreement, dictated by our interests and purposes, any traits of the explicans come under the head of "don't-cares." (Quine, 1960, §53, my emphasis)

After presenting his account of explication, Quine says, "philosophical analysis, explication, has not always been seen in this way" (Quine, 1960, p. 259). In a footnote he acknowledges Carnap and cites *Meaning and Necessity* as having seen explication correctly. We have seen however, of course, that there is an important difference in their accounts. Quine discusses the idea of explication in many places and he is very consistent in what he says about the subject. In an explication, we begin by determining which aspect of the existing use of a term we wish to preserve, then we propose a substitute that agrees with the existing term in these contexts. In the next section we will look at how their accounts of explication figured in the debate over analyticity.[16]

2.2 Explication and Analyticity

In the previous section we saw the differences between Carnap and Quine on explication. Both see it as a two step process, where the second step involves the introduction of a new notion which is meant to replace the existing notion. But the first stage is quite different. For Carnap all that we need to do at the first stage is understand the term well enough that we could roughly predict when a speaker of the language would apply it. This then serves as a guide when we introduce the replacing notion, but does not significantly constrain the second stage. For Quine on the other hand, it is not enough to merely come up with a similar, precisely defined concept. At the first stage, on Quine's view, we need to identify what it is, about the use of the original expression, that

---

[16] In his 1990 *Pursuit of Truth*, Quine discusses disquotation as a condition on a successful explication of the notion of truth. He says of the disquotational schema: "Moreover, it is a full account: it explicates clearly the truth or falsity of every clear sentence"(Quine, 1990, p. 93). In the 1995 work *From Stimulus to Science* (Quine, 1995, pp. 62–64), there is a discussion of giving an explication of the predicate "denotes." Here he considers disquotation as a condition on a possible explication. This preserves the feature of the ordinary notion that a term like "rabbits" denotes rabbits. He warns that this could lead to the Nelson-Grelling paradox if we are not careful, but then shows how Tarski avoids this by not having the denotation predicate be itself definable in the language. In both of these cases he identifies disquotation as what is to be preserved by the explication. In both cases the difficulty is in providing a definition which satisfies the disquotational schema without engendering contradiction. In any case, this is another example where Quine is thinking of *explication* as involving the preservation of some aspects of the use of the existing concept.

we intend to preserve. We are then constrained by this at the second stage. Our newly introduced term must agree with the existing one in these "favored contexts."

In "Two Dogmas ...," Quine poses the problem of explicating a notion of analyticity wider than logical truth. Such an explication should count not only "all bachelors are bachelors" as analytic, but also "all bachelors are unmarried." Quine concludes, at the time, that no explication could be given. Carnap, on the other hand, believes meeting this challenge is a very straightforward task. After all, we understand the concept of *analytic* well enough that we could correctly predict when a competent user of the term would apply it or not. We are then free to define as we wish an expression which is similar to this notion, but defined in a manner that is more to our liking. Carnap chooses to do this by using *meaning postulates* (or elsewhere *semantic rules*). Logically true statements follow from the logical rules alone, while the wider term *analytic* applies to anything that follows from the logical rules together with the meaning postulates. This achieves extensional similarity, but *not by identifying and preserving some aspect of the ordinary notion*. So while it satisfies Carnap's demands of an explication, it does not satisfy Quine's.

I suggested in Lavers (2012), that Carnap and Quine are completely talking past one another on the subject of *analyticity*. This is because, while each is addressing the question of whether the concept of analyticity can be successfully explicated, they each mean different things by *successfully explicated*, as we just saw. Carnap's explication in terms of meaning postulates is perfectly successful according to Carnap's criteria for a successful explication – the extension is similar after all. But, as following from meaning postulates *is not* a property of the explicandum, and as Quine requires identifying and preserving properties of the explicandum, according to Quine's account of successful explication it is a clear failure:

> Carnap's present position is that one has specified a language quite rigorously only when one has fixed, by dint of so-called meaning postulates, what sentences are to count as analytic. The proponent is supposed to distinguish between those of his declarations which count as meaning postulates, and thus engender analyticity, and those that do not. This he does, presumably, by attaching the label "meaning postulate." (Quine, 1963a, p. 404)

Interpreted as identifying a feature of our existing conception of analyticity which is preserved by the explication, Quine sees Carnap's explication as comically bad.[17]

---

[17] Neither Carnap nor Quine ever discusses the differences between their accounts of explication, and it seems overwhelmingly likely that neither had noticed them. For Carnap's part this is

Carnap wrote a response to Quine's "Two Dogmas ..." shortly after it came out. This was never published during Carnap's lifetime, but was included in Quine and Carnap (1990). Here it is clear that Carnap sees Quine's demand, that there be a feature of the use of the ordinary notion that is preserved, as confused. Carnap in this response repeatedly accuses Quine of confusing properties of the explicatum with properties of the explicandum:

> Later Quine says: "Semantic rules <determining the analytic statements of an artificial language are of interest only insofar as we already understand the notion of analyticity; they are of no help in gaining this> understanding" (op. cit., p. 34). This is the same obscurity again. The answer is the same too: we have an understanding of the notion of analyticity, in practice clear enough for application in many cases, but not exact enough for certain cases or for theoretical purposes. The semantic rules give us an exact concept; we accept it as an explication if we find by comparison with the explicandum that it is sufficiently in accord with this. It seems to me that this demand is fulfilled for the two concepts under consideration here with respect to the simple, limited language systems treated thus far: (1) for the concept L-truth as an explication of logical truth in the narrow sense, (2) for the concept, based on meaning postulates, of L-truths as an explicatum for analyticity, truth in virtue of meaning (in the broad sense). (Quine & Carnap, 1990, p. 431)[18]

Carnap is clearly saying that his explication of analyticity satisfies his own account of what constitutes a successful explication. Quine is looking for what is preserved between the explicandum and explicatum. That is, Quine is looking for a central property of the explicandum which is also a property of the explicatum. Carnap sees Quine a *confusing* properties of the explicandum with properties of the explicatum. While Carnap believes that the explicandum and explicatum should have considerable extensional overlap, they need not share any characteristic property in common. But Quine is not confused here, he is looking for what aspect of the meaning of our ordinary notion is *preserved* by Carnap's explication. Quine is applying his own standards of successful explication. It is just that neither is aware of the differences between their accounts of explication.

2.3 Analyticity

Given the analysis of the dispute between Carnap and Quine on analyticity presented in this section, an affirmative answer to Quine's question of whether

---

particularly understandable. After all, Quine tends to begin his discussions of how explications function by referencing Carnap's as having seen the matter rightly. Their not being aware of the differences in there views on explication led to misunderstandings of each others views on *analyticity*.

[18] The portion in angle brackets was added by Creath to Carnap's notes for the sake of the reader.

analyticity can be successfully explicated is strongly suggested. And this even relative to *Quine's account* of successful explication. Quine believes that for many concepts, it is clear, relative to our purpose and interests, what any explication of that concept ought to preserve. Now, there is a traditional connection between analytic truth and analysis. Analytic truths are, traditionally, truths discovered in the process of an analysis. This suggests that we take the features identified in the first stage of a Quinean explication (and what follows from them) as our analytic truths.[19] To use what Quine sees as the clearest example, it is an analytic truth that $\langle x,y \rangle = \langle w,z \rangle$ only if $x = w$ and $y = z$. It is not an analytic truth, however, that $\langle x,y \rangle = \{\{x\},\{x,y\}\}$. Notice that what is identified as a "favored contexts" in the analysis of one of our concepts could then be used to define the set of analytic truths in the manner that Carnap intended to do with *meaning postulates*.[20] The logical truths are consequences of the set of basic logical truths, while the analytic truths consequences of this set plus the set of "favored contexts" identified in the process of carrying out our various explications. Notice that Quine cannot reject this definition as he did Carnap's own appeal to meaning postulates. Remember, he dismissed Carnap's appeal to meaning postulates as ad hoc and artificial. But the distinction between "favored contexts" and "don't-cares" is central to Quine's understanding of a successful explication, and this in turn is, as Quine stresses in "Two Dogmas …," an important "activity to which philosophers are given, and scientists also in their more philosophical moments."

In the previous paragraph, I took logic to be given and I defined *analytic* as what follows logically from the *favored contexts* that we identify. But we would like to have logic itself be analytic in some non-trivial sense. To do this we just need that in the case of logical notions, what is identified as a favored context will include not just propositions but also rules of inference. I also want to be somewhat liberal here and allow for even infinitary rules of inference so that something like an ω-rule could be analytic. That is, I do not wish to limit the identified rule of inference to formal rules of inference, but wish,

---

[19] Burgess (2004) defines a notion that Burgess calls "pragmatic analyticity." Burgess defines this by stating, "My proposal is that the law should be regarded as 'basic', as 'part of the meaning or concept attached to the term', when in case of disagreement over the law, it would be helpful for the minority or perhaps even both sides to stop using the term, or at least to attach some distinguishing modifier to it" (Burgess, 2004, p. 54). While this may amount to the same thing, I believe that my notion of Quinean-analyticity is more clearly defined. I also think that connecting the notion of Quinean-analyticity to what Quine himself says about explications (analysis) shows more continuity with older conceptions of analytic truth. I was not yet aware of Burgess's paper when I wrote Lavers (2012).

[20] Remember I am using *favored context* to refer to what is identified as being what any explication ought to preserve.

following Carnap and the early Quine, to allow for analyticity to be defined so as to include a non-recursively enumerable set of analytic truths.[21] We then take as analytic the closure of the favored contexts under the identified rules of inference. One could accept a weaker notion of consequence and still accept the definition of analyticity provided here, but as I and others have argued in the works just cited, this will be insufficient for capturing our full understanding of mathematical truth. It is therefore straightforward to extend this account to one which allows logical truths to be analytic via an explication of logical concepts.[22]

One of the advantages of this definition of analytic is that it distinguishes between what is a conceptual truth from what is a purely stipulative truth. "$\langle x, y \rangle = \langle w, z \rangle$ only if $x = w$ and $y = z$" is something that we identify as an important conceptual truth about the notion of an ordered pair, while "$\langle x, y \rangle = \{\{x\}, \{x,y\}\}$" is something that is true (by stipulation) on one explication and false on others. This in turn can be used to address the main point of Benacerraf (1965). There Benacerraf argues against any particular set-theoretic explication of number, on the basis that such an explication will confer on number properties that are foreign to them. He imagines two children of diehard logicists named Ernie and Johnny. As a result of what must have been an oversight, Ernie uses *John* von Neumann's definition of the ordinals and Johnny uses *Ernst* Zermelo's. Ernie and Johnny then get into a disagreement over whether 3 is a member of 17. Ernie says it is, Johnny says it isn't. Here we see a disagreement about what is purely stipulative on one explication and false on another. In other words, this disagreement concerns only "don't-cares." The mathematically interesting properties of number are exactly the analytic properties of number as just explicated.[23]

This definition does not, of course, eliminate all the vagueness of the term *analytic*. Especially when considering sentences of natural language it may be

---

[21] I will not here defend the use of strong consequence relation here but merely point the readers to Kreisel (1967), Shapiro (1991), Warren (2020) and Lavers (2008, 2009).

[22] Of course, which rules are to be preserved on any explication of our logical concepts, will be a highly debated subject, and I won't settle the matter here. There is of course much to be said on the related subject of the status of logic and the identification of logical laws, but in the present work it will be assumed that we are working with an appropriate definition of logical consequence.

[23] In mathematics a new term may be introduced by stipulation. While the term used is somewhat arbitrary, this is not a case of arbitrary stipulation like the case of the specific definition of ordered pair that is used. If someone said, for example, a *surjection* is any function from one set onto another, this is an attempt to fix the meaning of a newly introduced term. Once this meaning is accepted a Quinean explication of the term would identify this property as being in the *favored context* for the concept of a surjection. As such this property would be preserved by all explications.

difficult to determine if they are analytic according to this definition. In one of his earliest expressions of serious doubt concerning the concept of analyticity, from a letter to Carnap in November of 1943, Quine writes, "Honestly I don't know whether 'Scott is human' is for me analytic or synthetic, nor whether 'human being' means the same as 'rational animal' " (Quine & Carnap, 1990, p. 367).[24] What is important though is, first, this analysis satisfies Quine's account of successful explication. And secondly, in mathematics, it tends to be completely straightforward to distinguish between the important properties to be preserved by an explication and the "don't-cares." For instance, Quine thinks it is completely clear what any satisfactory explication of number ought to satisfy. The same is obviously true of other mathematical concepts such as groups, rings or fields.

Quine famously wanted a *behavioristic* explication of analyticity, and the account of *analyticity* under consideration is clearly not given in behavioristic terms. But there are two things to be said of this. First behaviorism has significantly fallen out of favor and this demand is hardly one we see as appropriate for contemporary philosophical definitions. Second, not all explications which Quine views as successful meet this standard. Tarski's definition of truth, which Quine so often refers to as a successful explication, is not given in behavioristic terms. One might point out that it could be grounded behavioristically by tying it to what a speaker would assent to. But presumably Quine would have to hold that *analytic*, as here defined, must be in principle, explicable behavioristically. Since Quine thinks we can often distinguish between features of the use of a term which ought to be preserved by an explication and "don't-cares," then presumably Quine would hold that a field linguist observing us could come to understand this distinction as well.

As we saw, Quine does eventually accept several definitions of *analytic* (for a discussion of these see Creath 2007), but he is quick to point out that from these one may get statements of ordinary language, such as "there are seven days a week," counting as analytic, one does not get much more than this. In particular, Quine points out, that contra Carnap, it does not turn out that mathematics is analytic. "In short, I recognize analyticity in its obvious and useful but epistemically insignificant applications. The needs that Carnap felt for this notion in connection with mathematical truth are better met through holism"

---

[24] Although relative to our scientific purposes, "human beings are rational animals" is certainly not analytic in the sense defined in this section, but there remains quite a bit of vagueness when considering statements of natural language. That said, this Element is concerned with the analyticity of mathematics, and here this problem of the vagueness of terms is much less present.

(Quine, 2008, p. 397). This "epistemic insignificance" has to do with the specific definition of *analytic* that Quine was considering, a view different from the one suggested in this section. But I wish to defend the view that a definition of *analytic* based on Quine's distinction between *favored contexts* and *don't-cares* is perfectly suited to give an account of the analyticity of mathematics. Waismann in the late 1940s and early 1950s wrote a series of articles critical of the concept of analyticity.[25] Here he argued that analyticity is both vague and open-textured. He also, in this period, argued against reductionism. All that said, he maintained that in mathematics, everything is *perfectly* clear.

> In the [...] case of any purely mathematical truth, we can demonstrate it with all the rigour we may desire, and once we comprehend the proof, no obscurity is left, nothing that makes us ask the question "Why?" – everything is perfectly clear and transparent. (Waismann, 1951/1968, p. 164)

Waismann defended the view that mathematics is *tautological*. I will not follow Waismann on this point, but I certainly endorse the spirit of Waismann's observation that in mathematics what we mean is extremely clear, and much more so than in ordinary language. One ought to expect, then, contra the later Quine, that clear cases of *analyticity* or truth in virtue of meaning *will be more easily found in mathematics than in ordinary language*. In the next couple of sections I would like to consider what Quine says about the explication of the concept of natural numbers and sets, as he is quite explicit about these cases.

2.4 Arithmetic and Explication

We have now seen then how Quine takes explication to function and what he takes as the characteristics of a successful explication. Let us now turn our attention to what Quine says about explication and the philosophy of mathematics in particular. Quine is explicit in many places that it *is* possible to give a successful analysis of arithmetic. Quine defends Frege's definition of number against a family of objections. In analyzing numbers we identify laws which hold of any series any of whose members has only finitely many predecessors. Any sequence which satisfies these laws then would constitute a successful analysis of number – differing only concerning "don't-cares."

---

[25] See Lavers (2019b) for a further discussion of Quine and Waismann's views on this subject. We will come back to Waismann in the next section. We will look at Waismann on vagueness and open texture in the final section.

[N]othing needs be said in rebuttal of those critics, from Peano onward, who have rejected Frege's version because there are things about classes of classes that we have not been prone to say about numbers. Nothing, indeed, is more logical than to say that if numbers and classes of classes have different properties then numbers are not classes of classes; but what is overlooked is the point of explication. (Quine, 1960, §54)

Numbers can be explicated in various ways as sets. All of the various explications satisfy the arithmetical laws, so any difference between the explications, or between the explication and the ordinary notion point only to inessential features. In §54 of *Word & Object* Quine is clear that arithmetic lends itself to being explicated because we can so easily and clearly separate what must be preserved:

The condition upon all acceptable explications of number (that is, the natural numbers 0, 1, 2, ...) can be put almost as succinctly as [the condition on ordered pairs]: any progression i.e., any infinite series each of whose members has only finitely many precursors – will do nicely. (Quine, 1960, §54)

from "don't-cares:"

One uses Frege's version or von Neumann's or yet another, such as Zermelo's, opportunistically to suit the job in hand, if the job is one that calls for providing a version of number at all. (Quine, 1960, §54)

We find a similar point being made, if we look at "Ontological Relativity," from 1968:

What, after all, is a natural number? There are Frege's version, Zermelo's, and von Neumann's, and countless further alternatives, all mutually incompatible and equally correct. What we are doing in any one of these explications of natural number is to devise set-theoretic models to satisfy laws which the natural numbers in an unexplicated sense had been meant to satisfy. (Quine, 1969, p. 43)

Here what we wish to preserve are the laws of arithmetic. Any account from which we can derive the laws of arithmetic will be a successful explication, and differences between them (such as whether 3 is a member of 17) fall under the "don't-cares." In the case of arithmetic then, Quine does not think there is ambiguity about what is a conceptual truth of arithmetic, which ought to be preserved by any explication and a purely stipulative truth which is relative to a particular explication. Of course, as touched on earlier, although there is no problem for identifying the conceptual truths that any account of arithmetic must preserve, providing such an account must be done in set theory or type theory, and this is where Quine sees a limit to what can be done by explication. It is true, in this essay, Quine does say:

> Numbers in turn are known only by their laws, the laws of arithmetic, so that any constructs obeying those laws – certain sets, for instance – are eligible in turn as explications of number. Sets in turn are known only by their laws, the laws of set theory. (Quine, 1969, p. 44)

This quote seems to suggest a close connection between the cases of arithmetic and set theory. However, as we will see in the next section, Quine clearly does not take the phrase "the laws of set theory" to be univocal, as he clearly does in the case of "the laws of number." Let us now, then, turn to the subject of set theory.

2.5 Set Theory and Explication

We saw in the last section that Quine believed we could, in the case of arithmetic clearly distinguish the *favored contexts* from the *don't-cares*. As we will see in this section this is definitely not his view on set-theory. The case of set theory is interesting since so much of mathematics is expressible in set theory. Also, exploring the difference between Quine's view and Boolos is useful as I will be defending a position on the analyticity of mathematics which sides with Boolos, over Quine, on conception of the status of the axioms of set theory. In this section I will show what Quine's position is, show how Boolos objects, and then briefly give my reasons for siding with Boolos.

Quine saw the definition of various systems of set-theory as pragmatically very useful. If we have classes, then it is relatively unproblematic to explicate all the mathematical objects we wish:

> Classes can do the work of ordered pairs and hence also of relations (§53), and they can do the work of the natural numbers (§54). They can do the work of richer sorts of number too – rational, real, complex; for these can be variously explicated on the basis of natural numbers by suitable constructions of classes and relations. Numerical functions, in turn, can be explicated as relations of numbers. All the universe of classes leaves no further objects to be desired for the whole of classical mathematics. (Quine, 1960, pp. 266–267)

The question, then, that clearly suggests itself is whether we can successfully explicate the concept of *set*. Sean Morris, in his recent book on Quine and set theory (Morris, 2018), mentions one problem for this explication.[26] For Quine, explication is elimination, and there is no category of entities that suggest

---

[26] I discuss Morris on this point in Lavers (2021), but there I was limited to 800 words and so could only outline this argument.

themselves as candidates for sets to be explicated in terms of. As we saw earlier though, explication for Quine does not always involve ontological elimination. But apart from the problem of our inability to reduce sets to another kind of entity, Morris writes: "[s]till, I think explication is the right way to describe Quine's approach to set theory" (p. 174). However, Quine is clear that we *cannot* give an explication of set theory. The reason is that we cannot identify, from a central feature of the intuitive notion, a comprehension principle any which account ought to preserve.

We saw that Quine took Carnap's explications of analyticity to fail because he could not find in Carnap's explication a feature of the intuitive notion that the explication was meant to preserve. Concerning set theory Quine repeatedly states that, if we look to the intuitive notion of set, the only comprehension principle we can identify is naive comprehension. In the face of the paradoxes, Quine is quite clear that with respect to set theory, *intuition is bankrupt*, and as a result we must content ourselves with arbitrary and ad hoc restrictions on naive comprehension:

> It is not for nothing, after all, that set theorists resort to the axiomatic method. Intuition here is bankrupt, and to keep the reader innocent of this fact through half a book is a sorry business even when it can be done. (Quine, 1963b, p. x)

An explication begins by our identifying the central conceptual truths which we wish to preserve, and then we must come up with a clear replacement, which preserves the central features. If we cannot identify what it is about the original notion that we take to be worthy of explication and merely come up with a replacement, then the newly introduced replacement is purely ad hoc and not at all an explication.

In his book, Morris takes issue with Boolos's criticism of Quine's New Foundations theory of sets. In particular, Morris takes issue with this claim:

> ZF alone (together with its extensions and subsystems) is not only a consistent (apparently) but also an independently motivated theory of sets: there is, so to speak, a "thought behind it" about the nature of sets which might have been put forth even if, impossibly, naive set theory had been consistent. The thought, moreover, can be described in a rough, but informative way without first stating the theory the thought is behind. (Boolos, 1971, p. 219)

Morris takes issue with the "alone" at the start of this quote. It is clear that the point of Boolos's paper is not so much to defend the claim that all alternatives to ZF (including Quine's New Foundations, NF) lack independent motivation. In fact, this claim is supported by little else than a reference to Russell who said that no logician unaware of the paradoxes would ever have come up with Quine's system of NF. The main idea defended in the paper is that ZF *is* well motivated. I do not here want to address the main issue between Morris and Boolos over whether any independent motivation can be given for NF.[27] What I want to address next the issue between Boolos and Quine over whether ZFC is arbitrary and ad hoc and divorced from intuition, or founded on a natural and intuitive conception of set.

The point I want to make here is that the situation that Boolos describes in the beginning of his paper is very much an accurate description of Quine's view on set theory. Here is the opening of Boolos's paper where he lays out the position that he seeks to overturn.

> Faced with the inconsistency of naive set theory, one might come to believe that any decision to adopt a system of axioms about sets would be arbitrary in that no explanation could be given why the particular system adopted had any greater claim to describe what we conceive sets and the membership relation to be like than some other system, perhaps incompatible with the one chosen. One might think that no answer could be given to the question: why adopt this particular system rather than that or this other one? One might suppose that any apparently consistent theory of sets would have to be unnatural in some way or fragmentary, and that, if consistent, its consistency would be due to certain provisions that were laid down for the express purpose of avoiding the paradoxes that show naive set theory inconsistent, but that lack any independent motivation. (Boolos, 1971, p. 218)

The view here described only as what "one might come to believe" is not attributed to Quine. That said, I want now to show that this very much is Quine's view on the subject.

Let us begin with what Quine says about set theory in his 1939 piece "A logistical approach to the ontological problem." Here we see Quine clearly advancing the view that all responses to the paradoxes are merely ad hoc stipulations unsupported by intuition:

> The above phrase "every combination" is vague. We cannot, even in our transcendent universe, allow a new entity to be determined by every formulable condition on entities; this is known to lead to contradiction in the case of the condition "$\sim (x\epsilon x)$" and certain others. Such illusory combinations of entities can be ruled out by one or another stipulation; but it is significant that such stipulations are *ad hoc*, unsupported by intuition. (Quine, 1939/1976, p. 69)

---

[27] See Morris (2018) for a defense of the claim that NF is well motivated.

In his Mathematical Logic of 1940, Quine makes much the same point:

> The notion of membership is a natural object of suspicion; for it is this notion that imports the whole realm of classes of higher and higher orders of abstractness, and even calls for *ad hoc* measures such as the distinction between element and non-element for the avoidance of contradiction. (Quine, 1940, §60)

In his "Logic and the Reification of Universals," of 1947, Quine writes, "Classical mathematics has roughly the above theory as its foundation, subject, however, to one or another *arbitrary restriction*, of such kind as to restore consistency without disturbing Cantor's result" (Quine, 1948a, pp. 121–122, my italics). In "On what there is" of 1948, there is a very short discussion of set theory and Quine makes exactly the same point. "These contradictions had to be obviated by unintuitive, *ad hoc* devices; our mathematical myth-making became deliberate and evident to all" (Quine, 1948b, p. 18).

The discussion of sets from "Ways of paradox" is probably the best illustration of this attitude on Quine's part.

> But we cannot simply withhold each antinomy-producing membership condition and assume classes corresponding to the rest. The trouble is that there are membership conditions corresponding to each of which, by itself, we can innocuously assume a class, and yet these classes together can yield a contradiction. We are driven to seeking optimum consistent combinations of existence assumptions, and consequently there is a great variety of proposals for the foundations of general set theory. *Each proposed scheme is unnatural*, because the natural scheme is the unrestricted one that the antinomies discredit[.] (Quine, 1976, p. 18, my italics)

In Word & Object, Quine is quite explicit in holding exactly the kind of position that Boolos is attempting to refute. Remember, Boolos is arguing against the view that any consistent set theory is some kind of arbitrary contrivance made simply to avoid paradox. When he speaks of ways of coming up with consistent set theories Quine says:

> Naturalness, for whatever it is worth, is of course lost; a multitude of mutually alternative, mutually incompatible systems of class theory arises, each with only the most bleakly pragmatic claims to attention. Insofar as a leaning or tolerance toward classes may have turned on considerations of naturalness, nominalism scores. (Quine, 1960, §55)

So we see that Quine is incredibly consistent on this point. There is one natural comprehension principle for introducing sets and that is the naive comprehension principle. But given the contradictions we need to accept an unnatural, ad hoc, and unmotivated alternative. Quine clearly sees the case of set theory as bleak in a way that, for instance, the case of ordered pair is not. Sure there are mutually inconsistent explications of the ordered pair, but we can identify beforehand what is a non-arbitrary, intuitive/conceptual truth, about this concept which must be preserved by any explication. This is precisely what we can't do in the case of sets. If we come up with some set theory which avoids paradox, it has no intuitive motivation and is justified on "bleakly pragmatic" grounds. There is no way in this case to separate the principles which are conceptual truths about our concept of set.

I do not want to rehash Boolos's arguments against Quine's position. Boolos (1971), himself, does an excellent job of arguing that the axioms of Z (ZFC without replacement or choice) are true relative to the iterative conception. The iterative conception of set is the view that we start with a collections of individuals (if any) at the 0th stage and then we iterate the powerset operation through the ordinals. Any set which exists, first appears at some stage in this *cumulative hierarchy*. The cumulative hierarchy is then a structure relative to which the axioms of Z are true. Further axioms like replacement and choice are justified by their consequences. They entail intuitively correct statements and not obvious falsehoods. This is sometimes (e.g. Russell and Whitehead in the *Principia*) referred to as *inductive* evidence for the truth of these axioms.

The title of this Element is *Mathematics Is (Mostly) Analytic*. The reason for the qualifying word was just touched on in the previous paragraph. Some mathematical axioms are arrived a by an analysis of some existing conception. According to Boolos, this is true of Z but not the axioms of Choice and replacement. These latter axioms are arrived at inductively. There are undoubtedly many more examples of such inductively justified axioms in many sub-fields of mathematics. Such axioms as well as statements that require them for their proof do not count as analytic as I have defined it here (they are not arrived at by analysis or explication). That said, a great deal of mathematics does count as analytic in the sense defined in this Element. In particular we have seen that this applies to all of arithmetic and, as per Boolos, most of the axioms of ZF set theory.[28] Additionally even if the axiom of choice is not analytic according to the present account, a statement like "If **AC**, then **Zorn's Lemma**" would be.

---

[28] Some will point out that a countable infinity of sentences will be derivable from Z and a countable infinity of sentences will not be derivable from Z alone but will be derivable in ZFC. It might seem to follow that my talk of *mostly* then is unwarranted. I think there is a clear sense in which in which if most of our axioms are analytic in the sense defined here, then most interesting mathematical claims will be as well. But to avoid this problem, it is perhaps best to interpret the claim that mathematics is mostly analytic as the claim that most of the axioms of mathematics, together with their consequences, are analytic in the sense defined here.

2.6 Quine and Analyticity: Conclusions

We saw that Quine rejected Carnap's attempted explication of analyticity in terms of meaning postulates because it was purely, in his mind, an ad hoc replacement for the ordinary concept, and not, by Quine's standards, a proper explication. Quine, unlike Carnap, saw it as important, in the course of providing an explication of some concept, to identify *favored contexts*. That is, we must begin by identifying what it is about the concept which we wish to preserve. Carnap's meaning postulates were never intended to do this. We also saw that Quine's distinction between what we called *favored contexts* and *don't-cares* is exactly what is needed to identify, in a motivated and natural way, what Carnap called *meaning postulates*. When doing so, however, we do not arrive at a concept of analyticity exactly like Carnap's, but we get an account of analytic truth that separates conceptual truths from what is stipulated regarding *don't-cares*.

Concerning Quine's views on the analyticity and mathematical truth, we saw that Quine continued to hold that all of mathematics was analytic until right before "Two Dogmas ..." when he rejected the concept altogether. When he did allow some statements to count as analytic, he reverses his position. Some basic logic and statements like "there are seven days a week" count as analytic, but not much else. In particular, not very much of mathematics will count as analytic. That said, it was shown that in the definition of analyticity considered here, all of arithmetic counts as analytic, according to Quine's own pronouncements. Also if we reject Quine's views that all set theories with restricted comprehension are purely ad hoc and unmotivated, then most of the axioms of set theory can be seen as analytic as well.

3 Boghossian and Truth in Virtue of Meaning

In the last section I hope to have shown that Quine's reservations, about whether we can successfully explicate "analyticity," can be addressed. There is, however, another well-known and often discussed attack on the concept of analyticity. I am speaking of the view presented and defended in Paul Boghossian's "Analyticity Reconsidered" (Boghossian, 1996).[29] Boghossian does not want to do away with analyticity completely. Here, Boghossian distinguishes between an *epistemic* conception of analyticity and a *metaphysical* one. While he wishes to defend the epistemic conception, he wishes to reject the metaphysical conception as ultimately incoherent. As the account I wish to defend is not an epistemic account of analyticity, it may be thought that the arguments

---

[29] This position is further defended in Boghossian (2017).

Boghossian puts forward against the metaphysical view apply to my position. Concerning the metaphysical conception of analyticity, Boghossian says:

> Isn't it in general true – indeed, isn't it in general a truism – that for any statement S, S is true iff for some p, S means that p and p? How could the mere fact that S means that p make it the case that S is true? Doesn't it also have to be the case that p? (Boghossian, 1996, p. 364)

Concerning the metaphysical concept, Boghossian asks rhetorically "how can we make sense of the idea that something is made true by our meaning something by a sentence?" (Boghossian, 1996, p. 365). In this section, I would like to make sense of truth in virtue of meaning in the face of Boghossian's arguments. Before addressing Boghossian directly, however, I would like to discuss a much earlier attack on truth in virtue of meaning stemming from Waismann's series of papers on analyticity. There is a lesson to be learned from this episode, which I will then apply to Boghossian's arguments.

3.1 Waismann on Frege's "Mistake"

Between 1949 and 1953, Friedrich Waismann wrote a series of papers on the subject of analyticity. Overall he is quite critical of various attempts to define analyticity. He begins by considering suggestions on how to define analyticity. One suggestion he associates with Arthur Pap, who described analytic statements as statements whose truth follows from the meaning of the terms involved. Waismann expresses his sheer bafflement at this proposal:

> Here I immediately come up against a stumbling block: what can be meant by saying that a statement follows from the very meaning of its terms? I should have thought that one statement can follow from another; but from the meaning-! Yet, strangely enough, such a view has been taken by no one less than Frege. (Waismann, 1949/1968, p. 124)

Since Waismann mentions Frege here, I will address Waismann on Frege rather than Pap. The reason for this is that, in this case, the difference between the literal interpretation of Frege's words and what Frege actually meant can be clearly shown. With respect to the literal interpretation of Frege's words, Waismann is at a loss to see how any reasonable person could assert such a thing. "If [... someone] tells me that an equation follows from the meaning of its terms, or that an analytic statement is one whose truth follows from the meaning of its terms, I am absolutely at a loss to make head or tail of it" (Waismann, 1949/1968, p. 125). Despite Waismann claiming that Frege gave "not the slightest hint" of what he meant, if we dig just a little into what Frege meant here, we see that a straightforward interpretation suggests itself clearly.

Let us look at the passage that Waismann takes issue with. In this part of *Grundgesetze*, Frege is responding to Thomae who holds a formalist view of mathematics. In particular, that mathematicians lay down rules for symbol manipulation, but the assertions expressed should be seen as analogous to configurations on a chess board, and not really making an actual claim about any objects and their properties. Frege discusses this position in some detail and concludes by making the following claim:

> The rules follow in fact of necessity from the references [Bedeutungen] of the signs and these references are the actual objects of arithmetic; what is arbitrary is just the notation. (Ebert & Rossberg, 2013, §158)

So on the face of it, Frege is clearly putting forward the kind of view Waismann finds baffling. In fact, Frege's pronouncement here may be even more baffling, as he is speaking of the rules following from the *Bedeutungen* and not the *Sinne* of the expressions. Most who think of truth in virtue of meaning are thinking of truth following from the sense not the reference of expressions. However, if we look a little closer, we see that what Frege is doing is essentially standard practice for him. I will claim that an ounce of charity would avoid this problem, but I will get to that shortly, after a brief discussion of what is contained in these sections. Frege is trying to put forward a position which avoids the problems he sees with both a more classical conception of the real numbers and a modern formalistic one. The classical position defines real numbers as ratios of *spatial* magnitudes, and has the problem of not being able to explain the generality of the application of real numbers. For instance, Frege points out, masses and light intensities can take on any real value. Why should the laws of relations of *spatial* magnitudes apply to what is not spatial? On the other hand, the formalist position of Thomae, sees the laws of real numbers as not making any claim (true or false) about anything, and so has trouble explaining the applicability of the laws of real number *at all*. Frege's strategy is to define the identity of magnitude-ratios (of any kind) in terms of an identity between value-ranges. Frege explains the situation as follows:

> We have been reminded of our transformation of the generality of an equality into an equality of value-ranges that promises to accomplish what the creative definitions of other mathematicians are not capable of. We have understood the real numbers as magnitude-ratios and so excluded formal arithmetic in the sense described above. Thereby we have indicated magnitudes as the objects between which such a ratio obtains. (Ebert & Rossberg, 2013, §157)

Frege takes himself to have avoided the problems with the classical definition which is too closely tied to *spatial* magnitudes. At the same time, according to his definition, laws of real numbers do state facts concerning objects, and so his definition avoids the problem he sees with a formalist account. It is this that he wants to stress in the quote that Waismann is critical of. That is, Frege wants to insist that the laws are true of a range of objects (magnitudes). Frege is not making a significant philosophical error here, but merely speaking slightly imprecisely, and in a manner, as mentioned, that an ounce of charity ought to clear up. He does not really mean to say that certain propositions (or rules) follow from certain objects. What he obviously intends here is that the laws of real number (the rules he is speaking of), on his interpretation, concern objects, and they *follow from the constructive definitions he used to introduce the terms for such objects*. I take it to be completely clear that this is what Frege intended, and that he did not intend to assert that a certain entailment relation holds between certain objects and propositions. As I mentioned earlier and as we will see with a couple of examples subsequently, this was quite standard practice for Frege. With this clarification of what Frege intended, it is then Waismann who is making the mistake of not giving a sufficiently charitable interpretation of Frege's words here, rather than Frege making a baffling philosophical error.

When Frege speaks of certain rules following from the meanings of symbols, he quite obviously means following from the definition, which fixes the meaning of the term. I said above that this was fairly standard practice for Frege and we can see Frege making similar moves from very early on. Take, for example, this quote from *Begriffsschrift*, where Frege is discussing a proposition which serves to define a newly introduced symbolism:

> Although originally (69) is not a judgment, it is immediately transformed into one, for, once the meaning of the new signs is specified, it must remain fixed, and therefore formula (69) also holds as a judgment, but as an analytic one, since it only makes apparent again what was put into the new signs. (Frege, 1879/1967, §24)

Notice, in this quote, Frege speaks of the meaning of a sign being fixed by a definition and that this renders the proposition analytic. Although this proposition does not introduce any new objects, we see a close connection, in Frege's mind between the meaning of a symbol and the proposition which introduces it. What I am suggesting here is that this close connection between the meaning of a symbol and the definition which introduces it explains his slight misstep in talking about something following from the meanings when he intends to speak of something following from a definition.

Frege believed that in the construction of a system, of arithmetic for instance, even if we use our existing terms (e.g. *individual numbers*), the meaning of the terms are to be completely determined by the definitions which introduce them.

> We must explain that the sense in which this sign was used before the new
> system was constructed is no longer of any concern to us, that its sense is to
> be understood purely from the constructive definitions that we have given.
> (Frege, 1914/1979, p. 211)

Clearly, Frege sees a close connection between the meaning of the terms and the propositions which introduce them. So when he speaks of something following from the meanings [bedautungen] of the terms, this is not a major confusion on Frege's part, but simply shorthand for *follows from the propositions which determine the meaning of the term.*

Waismann is baffled by Frege's talk of something following from the meaning of a term. But if we see such talk as being shorthand for *following from principles which characterizes the meaning of a term*, then we see that there is no reason for any puzzlement. In his Waismann (1956/1968), Waismann sees the goal of philosophy as developing various important *insights*. I think it is somewhat ironic that Waismann's mistake of attributing an incoherent position to Frege, leads to an important insight on the question of analyticity. I take it that, in general, those who attack as incoherent the idea of truth in virtue on meaning, are making essentially the same mistake as Waismann. Any talk of somethings being *true in virtue of meaning, following from the meaning of a term* or *being made true by the meaning of a sign*, is always to be charitably interpreted as following from principles which characterize the meaning of a term. I take it that no one, if pressed for clarification, would hold that entailment relations hold between meanings and propositions.[30] In the next sections, I wish to discuss Boghossian and his distinction between what he calls the *metaphysical* and *epistemic* conceptions of analyticity. Boghossian finds the metaphysical conception mistaken and baffling, but wishes to defend an epistemic interpretation. With this clarification of the situation between Frege and Waismann in place, we can now turn to the principal target of this section: Boghossian's criticism of truth in virtue of meaning.

3.2 Boghossian and Metaphysical Analyticity

In his very well-known paper "Analyticity Reconsidered" (Boghossian, 1996), Boghossian distinguishes between what he calls *metaphysical* and *epistemic* accounts of analyticity. My plan here is not to straightforwardly defend one of these positions over the others. What I want to do is rather argue that separated from some confusions, the metaphysical view of truth in virtue of meaning is a view of analyticity much like the one discussed in the previous section.

---

[30] Well, I can't really speak for everyone.

The epistemic conception of analyticity, on the other hand, essentially begins with *this same* conception of analyticity, and then, I will argue, superimposes an epistemic dimension on top. This epistemic dimension would allow us to show, in principle, if the details could be worked out, that we can have a priori knowledge of analytic truths. But it is important to note that the way analytic truths are singled out does not depend on this epistemic superstructure.[31]

Let us begin with Boghossian on the distinction that is now our focus. He introduces it by saying that on his preferred interpretation of *analyticity*:

> "[A]nalyticity" is an overtly epistemological notion: a statement is "true by virtue of its meaning" provided that grasp of its meaning alone suffices for justified belief in its truth.

He then continues:

> Another, far more metaphysical reading of the phrase "true by virtue of meaning" is also available, however, according to which a statement is analytic provided that, in some appropriate sense, it owes its truth value completely to its meaning, and not at all to "the facts." (Boghossian, 1996, p. 363)

Concerning the metaphysical conception, Boghossian states that a defender will have to maintain that "our meaning p by S makes it the case that p." He then goes on to claim "this line is itself fraught with difficulty. For how can we make sense of the idea that something is made true by our meaning something by a sentence?" (Boghossian, 1996, pp. 364–365). This is the main argument against the metaphysical view. The main argument against what he calls the *metaphysical view* is that it is ultimately incoherent. There are two additional arguments that I will deal with shortly, but the principal objection is this one. Let us look at this now. How is the truth of some claim supposed to follow from our meaning what we do by a claim? Of course, this is exactly the objection which Waismann raised against Pap and Frege. And the response is the same too: anyone who seriously discusses something *following from* the meaning of a term, does not mean to posit novel entailment relations (or some new relation like entailment) between meanings and propositions, but, more charitably, means that a certain proposition follows from propositions which *characterize the meaning* of a term. Likewise, propositions which characterize the meaning of a term make certain claims true (that is, they entail them). These propositions which characterize the meaning of a term (or terms), would presumably fall under the *favored contexts* which were discussed in the last section. As

---

[31] Hofmann and Horvath (2008) also argue against Boghossian on metaphysical analyticity, but the arguments presented there are different from those contained here.

such, the metaphysical view, minus the confusion pointed out, amounts to the same position that was discussed in the last section.[32] I would not, however, call this a metaphysical conception of analyticity, but rather a semantic one.

But as just stated, beyond this Waismannian bafflement there are a couple of other arguments against the metaphysical conception of analyticity. One of the further problem, that Boghossian sees with the metaphysical view, is that it is tied to the analytic conception of necessity. The analytic conception of necessity is most closely associated with Carnap, and Carnap held, for instance in *The Logical Syntax of Language*, that "Necessarily-*P*," should be understood to be the same as "⌜*P*⌝ is analytic." After *Syntax*, Carnap became more tolerant of modal logic, but still held that there is a strong connection between necessity and logical truth. From our perspective, we can see Carnap as only ever wishing to interpret the modal operators as asserting logical necessity. We can also see that there are a range of other possible interpretations for these operators. But even if there are historical connections between the view that Boghossian is attacking and the analytic understanding of necessity, this connection is completely accidental. There does not seem to be anything preventing one from holding something resembling what Boghossian calls the *metaphysical* view of analyticity while rejecting the analytic theory of necessity. The only thing preventing such a view is that the metaphysical view is not a clearly defined position but a confused position associated with the view that entailment relations exist between meanings and propositions.

The other main criticism Boghossian offers for the metaphysical view is that it is too closely tied to conventionalism. Once again, it is true, at least in the case of Carnap, that there is some connection to conventionalism. Carnap, when discussing the principle of tolerance in *The Logical Syntax of Language*, talks of establishing conventions instead of setting up prohibitions. However, Carnap's ties to conventionalism are a lot weaker than much of the commentary on Carnap's work would suggest. Carnap saw certain conventionalist views, which he calls "radical conventionalism," as leading to a coherence theory of truth. When Carnap discusses conventionalism at all it is typically to distance his position (or those of allies like Poincaré or Neurath) from such radical views. Also,

---

[32] I have seen it happen on more than one occasion that an established philosopher (not always the same one) sets something of a trap for a younger philosopher. The established philosopher asks what makes it true that "it is either raining out or it isn't." The younger philosopher will begin to answer by talking about the meaning of disjunction and negation. The established philosopher will then chimes in with the much simpler answer that what makes it true is that it is, for instance, not raining out. But if instead of the unclear *makes it true*, we were to ask what are the (minimal) assumptions needed to demonstrate the truth of the claim, then the younger philosopher here is closer to giving what is required.

when Quine charges him of holding a conventionalist position with regard to logical truth, Carnap writes:

> Once the meanings of the individual words in a sentence of this form ["All black dog are dogs."] are given (which may be regarded as a matter of convention), then it is no longer a matter of convention or of arbitrary choice whether to regard the sentence as true; the truth of such a sentence is determined by the logical relations holding between the given meanings. (Carnap, 1963, p. 916)

Of course the position of conventionalism about the meaning of individual words is *universally accepted*. So, at least by the time of writing his responses for the Schilpp volume, Carnap held only an extremely weak form of conventionalism. Interestingly, notice that, in this quote, Carnap is guilty of misspeaking in the manner of Frege in the last section. When he speaks of "logical relation holding between the given meanings," he means to refer to logical relations which hold *given the propositions which characterize the meaning of the terms*. Additionally, of course, besides the question of how much of a convetionalist Carnap was, there is the question of whether anyone defending a metaphysical conception of the analytic needs to also hold some unacceptably strong version of conventionalism. I do not see why this would be the case.

Before turning to Boghossian on the epistemic conception of analyticity, there is one more point that I wish to address. This point is a rather a historical point, but an important one. In fairness though, Boghossian writes, "I should emphasize right at the outset, however, that I am not a historian and my interest here is not historical" (Boghossian, 1996, p. 361). That said, much of the article is a discussion of historical views. But there is one mistake on Boghossian's part that, I believe, merits correction, as it will come up again in a later section. In explaining how his own view does not amount to conventionalism, Boghossian writes, "I anticipate the complaint that the entailment between Implicit Definition and Conventionalism is blocked only through the tacit use of a distinction between a sentence and the proposition it expresses, a distinction that neither Carnap nor Quine would have approved" (Boghossian, 1996, p. 380). While it is true that that Quine as a "confirmed extensionalist" (see Quine, 2008), would never have accepted an account of propositions as individuated by their intensions, this is exactly what Carnap offers in *Meaning & Necessity*. Here Carnap even describes propositions as "objective, nonmental, extra-linguistic entities" (Carnap, 1947/1956, p. 25). It is, I believe too easy, and all too common to portray Carnap as somewhat dogmatically rejecting anything that seems too metaphysical. In truth however, Carnap is happy to accept such things as propositions once they can be given a sufficiently clear definition.

3.3 Boghossian and Epistemic Analyticity

In the previous section we saw that Boghossian rejects the metaphysical concept of analyticity. In part, this was because he takes the view to be incoherent, and in part because of associations with other views that have since fallen into disrepute. We saw the connections with other views in disrepute was completely contingent. More importantly, we also saw that we can eliminate the incoherence by interpreting *following form the meaning of terms* or *made true by the meaning of a term* as *following form principles which characterize the meaning of terms*. This leave us with a non-epistemic relation, and, in fact, the relation which I am calling analytic is of this type. If *C* is a useful concept and *P* is a proposition which characterizes the meaning of *C*, then *P* would be part of the *favored context* for this concept. That is, any explication of the concept would have to satisfy this principle. I would, as mentioned, not refer to this position as a *metaphysical* position, but rather as a *semantic* one. The main purpose of Boghossian's paper, however, is, not to attack the metaphysical view, but to *defend* the epistemic conception of analyticity. It is to this that we now turn.

As we saw, Boghossian states, with respect to the epistemic concept of analyticity that "a statement is 'true by virtue of its meaning' provided that grasp of its meaning alone suffices for justified belief in its truth" (Boghossian, 1996, p. 363). Obviously, this falls far short of being a clear and informative definition on its own (and, of course, is not put forward as such). Boghossian, therefore, considers ways of augmenting this suggestion in order to arrive at a more informative idea of the analytic. He first considers the notion of what is called Frege-analytic. A proposition is Frege-analytic if it can be transformed into a logical truth by substituting synonyms for synonyms. Concerning Frege-anlyticity, Boghossian writes:

> Now, it should be obvious that Frege-analyticity is at best an incomplete explanation of a statement's epistemic analyticity and, hence, of its apriority. For suppose that a given sentence S is Frege-analytic. How might this fact explain its analyticity? Clearly, two further assumptions are needed. First, that facts about synonymy are knowable a priori; and second, that the truths of logic are. Under the terms of these further assumptions, a satisfying explanation goes through. (Boghossian, 1996, pp. 366–67)

Notice that the main reason this is an incomplete account of a statement's epistemic analyticity is that Frege-analyticity is not an epistemic relation. If, for a moment, we suppose that synonymy is an objective relation between terms and entailment is an objective relation between propositions, then statements could be Frege-analytic without anyone ever knowing them. Boghossian himself repeatedly talks of working within a background of realism about meanings, so these assumptions seem appropriate here. We see that in filling in the details of his account of *epistemic analyticity*, Boghossian begins with a relation that is *not epistemic*, and then argues that we can *complete* it by assuming epistemic principles, which make all Frege-analytic truths knowable. "The question whether facts about the sameness and difference of meaning are a priori cannot be discussed independently of the question what meaning is, and that is not an issue that I want to prejudge in the present context" (Boghossian, 1996, p. 367). This is a major issue to set aside in arguing for an epistemic account of analyticity as it is what makes the account epistemic.

Now, as a matter of historical fact, Quine, in his last days of trying to arrive at a definition of synonymy (in order to define analyticity), found himself forced (see Verhaegh, 2018) to assume that we must be able to know if two terms are synonymous, if they are so. It was actually the problems involved in trying to make such an account workable that likely lead him to reject analyticity and synonymy altogether. In 1943, in a letter to Carnap, Quine writes that he has no idea whether *human* and *rational animal* are synonymous.[33] So, even if Quine, later, thought it important to assume we can know two terms are synonymous when they are so, this assumption was on shaky ground from the start. On the assumption that facts about synonymy are knowable, Quine would not have thought it was a problem to explain the analyticity of "all bachelors are unmarried." Quine, right up until his ultimate rejection of the concept of *analyticity* (and even after), maintained that were we to have an acceptable definition of *synonymy*, we could in turn define *analyticity*. So the assumption Boghossian makes here, we see, is exactly a principle that Quine himself thought we must accept if we are to provide a definition of synonymy (and ultimately analyticity). It is also a principle that is likely not true, or even if fairly widely discussed, there has never been a definitive argument in favor of this principle and lots of reasons to reject it. In 1949, Quine describes this principle, in a letter to Goodman (see Verhaegh, 2018, pp. 178–180) as a Tarskian *condition of material adequacy* on any explication of the term *meaning*. As Quine saw things, at the time, we face a trichotomy, either we can (1) successfully explicate meanings (and define their identity conditions via a definition of synonymy – *no entity without identity*, after all), or (2) we do away with talk of meanings, synonymy and analyticity, or (3) we continue to misleadingly talk

---

[33] As Putnam argues in Putnam (1975) and Putnam (1973), we ought to differ to experts when their expertise is relevant to fixing the meaning of our terms. Weiner (2020) argues that this should be extended even to vague terms like "bald" and "obese." With this in mind, I don't think anyone can really be in doubt over whether the meaning, that is the modern scientific meaning of "human" is *rational animal* – clearly it is not.

of meanings even though we can't successfully define their identity conditions. At the time, Quine was still holding out hope for the first alternative. Also at the time, Quine described Nelson Goodman as brave, but foolhardy for taking the second option.[34]

Boghossian says that Fregean-analyticity is incomplete as it does not explain how analytic truths are knowable a priori. It is also incomplete in the sense that it cannot explain the analyticity of such truths as "Everything colored is extended." Another problem is that logic is assumed by the notion of Frege-analyticity (logical truths are trivially Frege-analytic). In order to account for the possibility of an informative account of the *a priority* of logic, Boghossian appeals to the idea of implicit definition. He calls what can be shown to be true by appeal to implicit definitions Carnap-analytic. Appealing to implicit definitions could also explain the analyticity of sentences like "Everything colored is extended" which fail to be Frege-analytic. One of his main lines of argument here is that one can accept implicit definitions as an explication of analyticity without committing oneself to conventionalism or non-factualism. I will discuss the question of the non-factuality and conventionality of analytic truths in the next section, but right now, let me say a few things about Boghossian's account of *epistemic analyticity* now expanded to include what is both Frege-analytic and what is Carnap-analytic.

As we saw, in the case of Frege-analytic, the notion of synonymy is doing most of the work, and *synonymy* is not an overtly epistemic notion. What transforms this into an overtly epistemic account of analyticity is the principle that the synonymy of two expressions is knowable a priori. But notice, that while this principle plays the role of making the account overtly epistemic, it is not needed *to characterize which truths are analytic*. It is for this reason that I say the epistemic dimension of *epistemic analyticity* is a superstructure that sits atop a non-epistemic notion. At least this is the case for Frege-analyticity, but exactly the same thing can be said once the account is extended to include Carnap-analyticity. There is nothing particularly epistemic about Carnapian-analyticity. Boghossian would need some story about how the implicit definitions are a priori knowable in order to make this into an epistemic conception of the analytic. Perhaps the case can be made that what is Frege-analytic or what is Carnap-analytic can be known a priori. In the case of Frege analyticity, Boghossian explicitly sets aside the question of whether any synonymy relation is knowable a priori. In the case of what is true in virtue of implicit definitions (or Carnap-analytic), Boghossian writes:

---

[34] Again, see Verhaegh (2018, pp. 178–180).

It is quite correct that I have not attempted to show that the relevant facts about meaning cited in the premises are knowable a priori, although I believe that it is intuitively quite clear that they are. I have purposely avoided discussing all issues relating to knowledge of meaning-facts. My brief here has been to defend epistemic analyticity; and this requires showing only that certain sentences are such that, if someone knows the relevant facts about their meaning, then that person will be in a position to form a justified belief about their truth. It does not require showing that the knowledge of those meaning-facts is itself a priori (although, I repeat, it seems quite clear to me that it will be). (Boghossian, 2017, p. 602)

Here we see Boghossian again mostly avoiding the question, but I think this quote is quite telling in another respect. If we assume the premises can be known (perhaps even a priori), then the role of the epistemic agent in this *epistemic* account of analyticity is merely to perform a certain logical inference (usually just modus ponens) to the truth of the analytic claim. But this then means that the role of the epistemic agent in the account could be replaced by the notion of consequence. It is the assumption that we can know the premises which is doing the real epistemic work – and this is something Boghossian does not argue for. Again, beyond what is outright assumed about our knowledge of meaning facts, there does not seem to be anything *essentially* epistemic about the epistemic account of analyticity.

As Boghossian presents things, what is primary is the definition which holds that a claim is analytic if knowledge of its meaning is sufficient for knowledge of its truth. But this on its own is not a useful definition without giving any idea of how this is to work. It is telling that when giving a more detailed account of how this is possible, he appeals to principles which characterize the meaning of an expression (either by stating synonymy relations or via implicit definitions), argues that this is plausibly knowable a priori, and then shows how an agent aware of all this could come to know an analytic truth. But what this suggests is that what is primary is the non-epistemic relation between a set of propositions (or rules of inference) which characterize the meaning of an expression and an analytic claim.

In fact, one gets the impression from Boghossian that there are many radically different ways one might try characterize the notion of analyticity (even if not all are as successful). One might try to define it as a metaphysical notion, as an epistemic notion, or perhaps, as something else entirely. However, what I think comes out of all this is that all reasonable attempts to define *analyticity* agree that what is analytic follows from principles which are characteristic of the meaning of an expression. One might even say, any explication of *analyticity* will have to preserve this feature.[35] There are not then, radically different ways to characterize analyticity. There is not a metaphysical and an epistemic analyticity, and no one need explore if there is an aesthetic, ethical or mereological conception of analyticity. There is really but one conception of the analytic and it is a semantic concept.

Boghossian thinks it was an important mistake of early twentieth-century philosophers to prejudge that all necessary truths were a priori. Boghossian is at least in danger of assuming too close of a connection between the a priori and the analytic.[36] Boghossian suggests that any account of analyticity that is not "overtly epistemic" is in danger of being incoherent. That said, the epistemic component of his epistemic conception of analyticity is grafted onto a notion that is not epistemic and perfectly coherent. While he suggests associating the analytic and necessary truths too closely is a mistake, I would maintain that we need not assume anything from the outset of a link between the analytic and the a priori. In the next section I would like to look at the relations between analytic truths and other notions including stipulations of conventions, necessary truths, and regular truth. I will also explore what can said about analytic truths which make ontological demands.

4 Analyticity and Its Relation to Other Concepts

4.1 Analyticity, Stipulation and Content

The early twentieth-century view, associated most strongly with Carnap, was that analytic truths are true by stipulation and that they are void of content. Quine criticizes Carnap for maintaining there were different kinds of truths. Quine famously asserts in "Two Dogmas ..." that Carnap can only preserve his double standard on ontology by appealing to the analytic/synthetic distinction.[37] It is true Carnap maintained that analytic claims are void of content. For instance, in *The Logical Syntax of Language*, Carnap defines the content of a

---

[35] This is not to say that the analysis in the recent book is the only possible way of defining analyticity. Principles which characterize meaning and are identified in the process of giving a (Quinean) explication is one way to define the analytic truths, one that is particularly useful for philosophy and in particular the philosophy of mathematics. A more empirical way of defining principles characterizing the meaning of terms (the "connections between meanings" that Chomsky was talking about in the quote from the introduction) is possible as well. In any case to determine what is analytic requires some way of determining which principles characterize the meaning of the relevant expressions.

[36] In the postscript to Boghossian (2017), Boghossian considers whether all a priori truths are analytic and argues that they are not.

[37] Elsewhere, Lavers (2015), I have argued that this is unfair as an attack on the later Carnap, and I will not revisit those arguments here.

proposition as the set of its non-analytic consequences. If we accept such a definition, then analytic truths, including all of mathematics, are void of content. What I think this shows is that the question of whether mathematical truths, if analytic, are void of content, comes down to what we choose to mean by *content*. I will not settle question of what we *ought* to mean by content here. I will discuss Gödel's criticism of Carnap on exactly this point. We will see that both Gödel and Carnap thought of mathematics as following from conceptual truths. What I take this to show is that the view defended here is compatible with both Carnap's and Gödel's positions. While I am quite sympathetic to Gödel's arguments here, without a definition of content, there is no way to take a side on this issue. The important point is that the claim, then, that mathematics is analytic (in the sense of this Element) is not equivalent to the claim that it is *tautological*, empty, or devoid of meaning.

Before turning to Gödel's criticism of Carnap, I would like to address the question of whether the view I am defending amounts to holding that mathematics is true by convention or stipulation. First of all, it can be straightforwardly pointed out that the way *analytic* has been defined here, it is not *identical* to what might be stipulated. Recall Quine's example of the ordered pair:

(1) $\langle x, y \rangle = \langle w, z \rangle$ only if $x = w$ and $y = z$

is identified as what must be preserved by any analysis of ordered pair. In my terminology this and what follows from it are called analytic.[38] We might stipulate that the ordered pairs are to be defined as per Kuratowski, but this stipulation is stronger than what I have identified as analytic of ordered pair. So, what is analytic and what is stipulated are at least not identical. Furthermore, we can ask if (1) is a matter of convention or stipulation. Here we have to be a little more careful. Of course, the meaning we associate with the particular marks "ordered pair" or "< , >" is a matter of convention. But it does not seem right to say that it is purely a matter of stipulation that an ordered pair must satisfy (1). For, if one were to stipulate a definition of "ordered pairs" which does not satisfy (1), that may be a proposed definition of "ordered pairs," but it would fail to introduce ordered pairs. If this is right, then that ordered pairs satisfy (1), is not a stipulative truth but a conceptual one. So what I am calling *analytic* is neither identical with, or even a subclass of purely stipulative truths.

---

[38] Notice it is the theory, and not merely what we identify as "favored contexts" that counts as analytic. Different "favored contexts" which generate the same theory give an equivalent set of analytic truths. So no Quinean argument about Ohio not having starting points can be used against analyticity as so defined.

Let us now turn to Gödel's criticism of Carnap on the question of whether mathematical sentences have content. Gödel, after having already made contributions to the Schilpp volumes on Russell and Einstein, agreed to contribute an article for the *Library of Living Philosophers* volume on Carnap. Gödel wanted to show that Carnap's positivistic "syntactical" interpretation of mathematics failed to do justice to how mathematics is actually used in the sciences. He produced six drafts of the work, over six years, but in the end none were to his satisfaction and he withdrew from the project. The third draft, the most complete, argues for two main points. The first concerns Carnap's overly liberal interpretation of what is to count as "syntactic." The second major point Gödel wished to establish, which is more relevant to our concern here, was that Carnap's definition of "content," begs the question in favor of a formalistic interpretation of mathematics:

> *Mathematical sentences have no content* only if the term "content" is taken from the beginning in a sense only acceptable to empiricists and not well founded even from the empirical standpoint." (Gödel, 1995a, p. 337)

Concerning how Carnap uses the term "content," Gödel writes:

> It can be shown [...] that *the reasoning which leads to the conclusion that no mathematical facts exist is nothing but a petitio principii, i.e., "fact" from the beginning is identified with "empirical fact," i.e., "synthetic fact concerning sensations."* In this sense the voidness of content can be admitted, but it ceases to have anything to do with the philosophical questions mentioned [...], since also Platonists should agree that mathematics has no content of this kind. (Gödel, 1995a, p. 351, original italics)

Gödel takes it that one of the central tenets of the syntactic interpretation of mathematics is that, in mathematics and its application in the sciences, one needs never appeal to our intuitive understanding of the standard models of our theories. To assume that we can know and speak meaningfully about the standard model is, in Gödel's view to abandon the syntactic approach. He argues that without appeal to the intuitive model we have no reason to see the mathematical theories we use in the sciences as consistent. We could still treat them as stipulations, but then by their not leading to false empirical consequences, we obtain inductive evidence of their consistency. Gödel stresses that when we test a theoretical claim we are always assuming a great deal of mathematics. It is then only ever *both* mathematics and physical theory that get tested. "If mathematical intuition is accepted at face value, the existence of a content is evidently admitted. If it is rejected, mathematical axioms become open to disproof and for this reason have content" (Gödel, 1995a, p. 348). Given this parallelism between theoretical and mathematical claims, Gödel argues it is question begging to declare that theoretical propositions have content, but mathematical claims are contentless.

We see in this criticism an opposition between Gödel, who rejects the claim that mathematics has no content, and Carnap who has defined content in a manner such that analytic claims, by definition, are contentless. So it seems the question of whether mathematics is empty or contentless, will turn on what we mean by *empty* or *content*. That said, both Carnap and Gödel hold quite similar views about the role of meaning in determining mathematical truth. That is, they both hold that the meaning of mathematical expressions is determined by fixing the meaning of the individual words, and the rest is a consequence of this. Recall the passage from Carnap's reply to Quine in the Schilpp volume (quoted earlier):

> Once the meanings of the individual words in a sentence of this form are given (which may be regarded as a matter of convention), then it is no longer a matter of convention or of arbitrary choice whether to regard the sentence as true; the truth of such a sentence is determined by the logical relations holding between the given meanings. (Carnap, 1963, p. 916)

Compare this to a remark from Gödel's unpublished draft IV of his "Is mathematics syntax of language?:"

> §42 It is interesting to note that, even disregarding the question of consistency, mathematics, also in syntactical interpretation, is not a bit more "conventional" than the factual sciences. For, in the latter, what is conventional is solely which symbols are used and which meanings are associated with them; once these conventions have been made, the truth or falsehood of sentences is objectively determined. But the same is true for mathematics also in case it is interpreted syntactically. For it is exactly by the rules of syntax that the meaning of the mathematical symbols is defined. But these rules, moreover, assert implicitly the existence (or the consistency) of those meanings and therefore have content[.] (Gödel, Unpublished 1953-9, quoted form Lavers 2019a)

So both Carnap and Gödel hold that mathematical truths are analytic in the sense of following from the propositions which fix the meanings of the individual terms. Gödel, however, wanted to stress that mathematics ultimately rests on conceptual truths:

> I wish to repeat that "analytic" here does not mean "true owing to our definitions," but rather "true owing to the nature of the concepts occurring [therein]," in contradistinction to "true owing to the properties and the behaviour of things." (Gödel, 1995b, p. 321)

This is very much in line with the view of analyticity proposed in this Element. Gödel is here stressing that mathematical truths are conceptual truths, as opposed to being merely stipulated by definition. One could define the *content* of a claim as content concerning the world of sensory experience, or one could define content more broadly so that mathematical claims have content. Without such a definition, there is no way to decide the matter between Gödel and Carnap. The focus of this Element is on the analyticity of mathematics, and I will not be putting forward a definition of content. The goal of the present section is to argue that whether mathematical claims have content or not is not decided by the present account of analyticity. Nothing about the claim that a sentence is analytic, in the sense defended in this Element, implies that such sentences are empty or tautological. All this said, Gödel clearly wants to hold that conceptual truths are not only contentful but true in a robustly realist sense. He says in "Is Mathematics the Syntax of Language" that the fundamental question of philosophy is how we can begin by reasoning about concepts and end up with objective knowledge of a range of objects. We will, in the next section, turn our discussion to the question of the sense in which conceptual truths are true, and in the following section we will deal with the ontological implications of analytic propositions.

4.2 True in Virtue of Meaning and True

I have argued that a truth of arithmetic, for instance, follows from what is analytic of our concept of number. I have also argued that the bafflement, which Waismann expresses faced with "Frege's mistake," is essentially the same incoherence which Boghossian sees in the notion of something "made true by our meaning something by a sentence." Talk of truth following from meaning, or of something "made true" in virtue of what we mean, has always, reasonably interpreted, I contend, meant following from principles which characterize the meaning of a term. But so far this does not add up to *truth* in virtue of meaning. If what is analytic of the concept of number characterizes the meaning of this concept, what reason do we have for thinking these express truths? If the basic principles which characterize the meaning of arithmetical expressions are not themselves true, then what follows from them has no right to be described as true in virtue of meaning. Boghossian, for instance, says that the only answer we can give to what makes anything true is something like *the world*. It follows from what I have said so far that anything we view as a truth of arithmetic is analytic, nothing I have said so far implies that they express truths. Nominalists like Hartry Field (Field, 1980) have argued that such claims are false. Fictionalists, like Mary Leng (Leng, 2010), believe that all mathematical statements on their straightforward interpretation are false, even if they are "true according to the story of mathematics." Such philosophers may be happy to admit that statements of arithmetic are analytic in the sense defined here, but would clearly reject any claim that these claims are *true* in virtue of meaning. That is, nominalists and fictionalists may admit that any analysis of the concept of number would have to satisfy the laws of arithmetic.[39] They may also not object to many statements being logical consequences of what we take to be true of our concept of number. What they object to is our calling what is true, on any analysis of our concept of number, *true*.

Are we not back then to saying that ultimately, it is *the world* that makes any claim true? This is certainly as Boghossian sees the matter. I believe we can defensibly say that the truths of arithmetic are *true* in virtue of meaning. The account of analyticity I have been putting forward is based on Quine's conception of an explication. But now we are asking about the truth of these analytic claims. To deal with this problem, I will begin by outlining a relativized notion of truth. Note that the mere acceptance of this relativized version of truth does not commit one to the *thesis of relativism*. That is, one can talk of truth in this relativized sense without rejecting a univocal (absolute) conception of truth. I want use this relativized notion of truth to analyze the problem of certain things which are conceptual truths regarding the concepts involved, but which are generally considered false. Such cases seem to be the primary motivation for claiming that not all conceptual truths are true. But I will argue that whether or not we accept some univocal conception of truth, these do not pose an insurmountable problem for the current view.

So far, in the previous sections, we have seen that analytic claims are conceptual truths of sorts, that are not purely stipulated or conventional. The account of analyticity presented is built on top of Quine's distinction between what must be preserved by any explication ("favored contexts") and the "don't-cares." This distinction Quine takes to be important, and in many cases completely clear. But the distinction is relative to our purposes and interests. So we end up with a somewhat relative notion of analytic that is ultimately founded on something pragmatic rather than something absolute. I believe it is this pragmatism that can answer one of the problems that faces any account of "true in virtue of meaning;" namely, is everything that is *true in virtue of meaning* true? One obviously faces a lot of *bad company* objections here. For instance, is it

---

[39] Hartry Field, Field (1994, 1998), has argued that what is or is not a consequence is highly indeterminate. I, Lavers (2008, 2009), and others, for instance Kreisel (1967), Shapiro (1991), have argued that the situation is not as dire as Field suggests and the use of informal methods and strong consequence relations are legitimate, and I will not discuss this further here.

not true of the logical notion of set held by Frege and Russell around the turn of the twentieth century, that every expressible property determines a set? This would seem to be a case of something that is *true in virtue of meaning* but not *true*. Many might also point to such examples as conceptual truths of phlogiston theory (e.g. "combustion is dephlogistication"). Others may ask about the status of the conceptual truths in logical system which includes a tonk operator. Presumably there are many examples of things that are true in virtue of meaning in a certain context, that we, from our perspective, think of as simply false. Such examples would seem to be a problem for the type of view considered in this Element.

I do not think such problems are a substantial hurdle for the view under consideration. As the account of analyticity defended here is based on a Quinean distinction, I think it is somewhat fitting that my answer to this difficulty will be appealing to pragmatism (and, perhaps, holism). No matter what, we are going to employ a range of concepts in our understanding of the world. Any such range of concepts used by a group at a particular time, I will call their conceptual scheme. Given a conceptual scheme S, we can define the notions of *analytic$_S$*, *background$_S$* and *true$_S$*. *Analytic$_S$* includes everything that is analytic in the sense under consideration for that group at that time, we will assume that some set of inference rules count as analytic too, and so, this includes a notion of consequence. *Background$_S$* would include everything *analytic$_S$*, but also all sorts of other background assumptions: things that are straightforwardly stipulated, as well as, perhaps, certain theoretical assumptions. *True$_S$* would include *background$_S$*, as well as all sort of claims accepted on the basis of experience. So, in particular, anything *analytic$_S$* is *true$_S$*. That is, those who have *background$_S$* take every proposition in *background$_S$* to be true. To take a simple example, anyone who shares our conceptual scheme, takes it as true that Wednesday comes immediately after Tuesday. So anything *analytic$_S$* is "true in virtue of meaning" in at least the (relativized) sense of *true$_S$*.

Now it could happen that a certain set of background assumptions *background$_S$* lead those who hold these assumptions into an incoherent position. On the basis of *background$_S$* and other claims that are *true$_S$*, it follows that some claim P is true, but at the same time, given the background we have reasons to hold that P is false.[40] When a group finds themselves in any incoherent

---

[40] Although I am not myself defending dialethism, I do not want to rule it out a priori. The dialethist would claim that there is a natural and pragmatically useful conceptual scheme that tolerates some inconsistencies. However, allowing for this makes it harder to define when one has an incoherent conceptual scheme. I will mostly talk of taking some claim to be both true and false as incoherent, but here just make the caveat that this may in some situations perhaps not be incoherent.

position, they will have to make changes somewhere in their set of assumptions background$_S$. There is, of course, no reason that conceptual truths are immune from revision, but to abandon a conceptual truth which characterizes a concept is to abandon that concept.

Let us assume that at some time before, a group with conceptual scheme B (for before) took some statement P to characterize the meaning of a certain expression. To take something of a more concrete example, let us say that those with conceptual scheme B are those that toward the end of the nineteenth century held the logical notion of set. As has been often pointed out (Grattan-Guinness, 2011, chapter 3), Cantor, for instance, did not share these assumptions, but let us consider our community small enough such that all members accepted the principle of naive comprehension P as analytic of their conception of set. This group saw sets as defined by a rule which separates *everything there is* into those things which satisfy the rule and those things that don't, with there being a set corresponding to each side of such a division. So, P expresses something which is *analytic$_B$* and thus *true$_B$*. But of course this puts members of this group in an incoherent situation. Once a set-theoretic paradox is discovered, given the logic they accepted at the time, anything becomes provable. From our perspective now we accept a conceptual scheme N (for now), which is incompatible with P. We say that P is false, but this is to say that P is *false$_N$*. Now, likely some, at this point, will object that P is not just false in some relative sense, but false simpliciter as it leads to a contradiction.[41] In opposition to this it can be pointed out that, for instance, moving to rough set theory, or accepting a dialethic logic could allow us to preserve naive comprehension while avoiding an incoherent position. That is, even if we modify our conceptual scheme by abandoning P, this does not imply that P is false in some absolute sense. A change has to be made somewhere to the background once those who share that background are in an incoherent position, but no particular change is forced on this group. One can insert the Neurathean sailor metaphor at this point. We can discover inconsistencies in our conceptual scheme, we can alter our conceptual scheme, but there is completely neutral perspective (no dry dock) from which we can evaluate the truth of any principle which characterizes a concept.

So far we have a picture according to which, at any time, we have a set of background assumptions, and included in this background are certain conceptual or analytic truths. Relative to each of these background assumptions there

---

[41] Boghossian's tact (see Boghossian 2003) is to rule out *defective* concepts. I, however, would suggest that it is it is conceptual schemes rather than individual concepts that are defective (what I am calling incoherent).

is a concept of truth. Nothing so far has been assumed about whether or not there is a non-relativized concept of truth. It certainly makes sense to compare various backgrounds to a degree. While we always have some freedom in how we alter our system of background beliefs, I do not wish to suggest that all ways of altering our background are on par. We can say that one set of background assumptions leads to incoherence in a way another set does not. We may also say that parts of our former background, including some (former) conceptual truths, are no longer tenable, given our changing state of knowledge. Perhaps, one might argue, there is an ideally coherent and complete set of background assumptions which would allow us to *best* describe the world. Truth simpliciter would then be truth relative to this ideal background. I do not want to take any position on the existence (or uniqueness) of such a background, which could be used to make sense of truth in an absolute sense. I am though, more inclined to look at a background as a set of tools used to try to come up with a more or less complete and coherent description of the world. We accept certain conceptual truths for their utility and we abandon the concepts relative to which they are conceptual truths when they lead to some kind of incoherence, or otherwise no longer seem useful.

Even if one is inclined to accept that there is a univocal conception of truth simpliciter, of which I am at least somewhat dubious, then all this means is that something's being a conceptual truth of our current conceptual system is only a fallible indicator of truth. We would just have to accept that certain things, which are conceptual truths in our current conceptual scheme may in fact be false (in the absolute sense). In the last section we looked at the question of whether the analyticity of mathematics implied that mathematics was devoid of content. We saw that this depended on what one means by "content." Carnap gave a definition of "content" as the non-analytic consequences of a claim. Gödel saw this as question-begging against the Platonist. That said, both held the view that mathematics was ultimately various conceptual/analytic truths and the consequences of these. So we saw that with the same conception of analyticity, there is a spectrum of positions one might take on the question of whether mathematics has content. Likewise on the question of relativism, we can once again see Carnap and Gödel representing opposing ends of a spectrum. Carnap stresses our freedom of choice in choosing a conceptual scheme and holds that analytic truths (in his sense – containing both analytic truths in my sense together with stipulations) are selected or discarded on pragmatic grounds. Gödel, representing the other end of the spectrum, believes that although our conceptual knowledge is fallible, mathematics, which is based on conceptual knowledge, still concerns an objective world of truth:

This [that our knowledge is to a degree indistinct] occurs in the paradoxes of set theory, which are frequently alleged as a disproof of Platonism, but, I think, quite unjustly. Our visual perceptions sometimes contradict our tactile perceptions, for example, in the case of a rod immersed in water, but nobody in his right mind will conclude from this fact that the outer world does not exist. (Gödel, 1995b, p. 321)

We saw previously that both the claim that mathematics is in some sense without content, and the claim that it does have content are compatible with the claim that mathematics is (mostly) analytic in the sense discussed in this Element. This comes down to how we define *content*. Likewise, both the views that mathematics is true only *relative* to a conceptual scheme, or that it is true in a more robust, realist sense is compatible with the account of analyticity now under discussion.

If relativism is true, that is there is no univocal conception of truth, then we can only talk about the usefulness and coherence of a conceptual scheme. We can say that one conceptual scheme is open to a certain incoherence, or that it is less useful than another. But there is no perspective here to judge the absolute truth or falsity of things which are true on a particular conceptual scheme. If there is a univocal conception of truth, then this only forces us to be fallibilists about our conceptual truths. One might ask, at this point, for the justification of the claim that something is a conceptual truth of our current conceptual scheme is an indicator of truth *at all*. Why might not most or all of our conceptual truths be false if there is a univocal concept of truth? Here I would just say that if the univocal conception of truth shares little in the way of conceptual truths with our own conception of truth, then it might be unreasonable to judge what is true in our background according to its agreement with that background presupposed by the univocal view. Also, we have done quite a bit of work in formulating useful concepts and eliminating incoherence. If a concept is useful, why should it not be included in an ideal background? This seems especially the case in mathematics. We may still have some incoherence to purge from our conceptual scheme, but it seems there are a lot of useful concepts in there too. Others may be more pessimistic than this, but I think this strong pessimism would require strong argument.

It should be noted that, even if mathematics is relative to a certain conceptual scheme, this does not imply that it is therefore mind or language dependent. We saw earlier that Carnap after defining propositions, states that propositions are objective, non-linguistic, extra-mental entities. The reason he says this is that we do not figure in the truth conditions for claims involving propositions. This means that, for instance, even on a Carnapian view, which would be a form of a relativist position, we can still say that mathematical claims express (objective) propositions, and that since we do not figure in the truth conditions for mathematical sentences, what the propositions assert does not depend on us. Carnap might have claimed that this does not amount to Platonism, as Platonism employs a metaphysical conception of reality. However, it should be pointed out that, as we saw, even according to Carnap's relativist position, mathematical propositions state truths that are independent of us (as we do not figure in their truth conditions). It is not clear what more a realist could ask for.

4.3 Analyticity and Ontology

In his 1939 paper "A Logistical Approach to the Ontological Problem" Quine formulates a way of asking ontological questions, which are not relative to the language system one is working in. If ontological questions are always relative to a language system, then all we can say is that a certain language system includes talk of real numbers, for example, and another system does not. Quine there famously identified the quantifiers as identifying the ontological commitments of a language. Quine then argues that we could ask, for any type of entity, whether we would need to quantify over that type of thing in a complete scientific description of the world. Is it possible, for instance to give a scientific description of the world that does not quantify over real numbers? This is now a question that is not tied any one language system. "How economical an ontology can we achieve and still have a language adequate to all purposes of science (Quine, 1939/1976, p. 68)?" At the time, Quine hopes to demonstrate the nominalist thesis that quantification over abstract objects is not needed for a scientific description of the world. This formulation of ontological questions, as well as the project of nominalism, was clear enough to satisfy Carnap. Of course, Carnap famously objects to the use of the term "ontology," for its ties to medieval metaphysics. That said, this is merely a terminological dispute, and Quine's approach to ontology and his definition of the nominalist program proved very influential.

This approach to ontology, although not universally accepted, is now standard. For all kinds of ontological questions, we can ask whether a complete scientific description of the world (regimented in first-order logic) would need to quantify over the entities that interest us. As I have argued elsewhere (Lavers, 2015), I see two main problems with this Quinean approach to ontology. The first main problem is that this approach to ontology leads to a plethora of unpromising research programs. For every type of entity, given that we have no idea what the best version of our scientific theories (regimented in first-order logic) will look like, both the positive and negative answer to Quine's ontological question for that type of entity are defensible. Those in support of a certain kind of entity can write a few papers pointing to the usefulness of talking of some kind of entity, and pointing out how the opponent has not yet showed that talk of this kind of entity is dispensable. The philosopher opposing talk of a certain kind of entity can point to the ontological economy of rejecting the entity in question, can make the case that not all that much overall simplicity is gained by commitment to the type of entity, and can give a sketch of how the elimination of talk of such entities might be carried out. Never is there a complete knock out blow from either side. Olympic sized swimming pools could be filled with papers which amount to little more than speculation over whether a future ideal science would need to talk of a certain kind of thing.

The second problem is a misunderstanding of Quine's explication of *ontology*. That this was intended as an explication is clear from Quine's remark: "I suspect that the sense in which I use this crusty old word has been nuclear to its usage all along" (Quine, 1951/1976, p. 127). How economical our ontology can be while still being adequate for science is meant to *replace* the question of what are the ultimate components of reality. Too many contemporary philosophers, working within the framework of a Quinean approach to ontology, think that via indispensability arguments together with a holistic attitude toward science, we get an answer to the traditional ontological questions. If for instance, sets or real numbers are indispensable for science, then these entities must be part of the ultimate constituents of metaphysical reality. We get an answer to the metaphysical question via science.

Whatever the value of much of the contemporary debate about ontology, although Quinean inspired, it is not Quine's view. In "Carnap's views on ontology" Quine begins emphasizing that he is "no champion of metaphysics." Carnap did not like Quine's use of the term *ontology*, but, as we saw, Quine takes himself to have explicated the term. He has therefore replaced traditional ontological questions with a clear counterpart. For Quine, the usefulness of mathematics in the physical sciences is not evidence for some metaphysical claim about the ultimate existence of mathematical objects. Ultimately Quine has a deep-seated pragmatic attitude. Quine does not think we can appeal to his holism to say that the entities presupposed by our best scientific theories probably correctly reflect the ultimate constituents of the world. Quine has replaced the traditional ontological question of concerning the ultimate constituents of reality with the ontological question as he defined it. But too much discussion accepts the broad framework of the Quinean position, but then tends to think that somehow we can take an answer to Quine's ontological question as *evidence* for the metaphysical question.

On these points, I am inclined to follow Quine's more pragmatic attitude, and deny that anything, of a metaphysical nature, follows from pragmatic questions about ontology. That the world is best described by a system which includes, let us assume, the real numbers, tells us no more than that our best description of the world includes real numbers within the scope of our quantifiers. We choose a conceptual scheme which suits our needs. If we run into incoherence we change our conceptual scheme. Obviously this position is in the end quite Carnapian (in the sense of Carnap 1950a).[42] If we are to be pragmatists about conceptual schemes, we can ask about the pragmatic value of such a framework or we could possibly expose an incoherence, but the question of the correctness of a conceptual scheme is rejected.

One might, following Quine's lead, object that while I talk of conceptual schemes as useful tools, I have not shown that to use a certain concept is a mere *façon de parlé*. Quine thought that this could be done only if we show how we could do without a concept in a complete scientific description of the world. Carnap thought analytic claims make no claims about the world. As I am not committed to holding that analytic truths are empty or tautological, I need not show that conceptual truths tell us nothing about the world. But, again, what the use of real numbers in our best scientific theories tells us about the world is that it is best described in a scientific language which includes the laws of analysis among its conceptual truths. I see no reason to conclude more than this.

5 The Analyticity of Mathematics: Final Thoughts

5.1 Vagueness and Analyticity

It is certainly true that, for many concepts, it will be very difficult to identify what is analytic of them. As Bertrand Russell said, "Everything is vague to a degree you do not realize till you have tried to make it precise (Russell, 1918/1956, p. 180)[.]" Of course there are terms in language like *tall* and *bald*, for which we are often unsure of the exact range of applicability. If analyticity is truth in virtue of meaning, and meaning is often not clear enough to determine clearly the applicability conditions for a term, then is analyticity as I have

---

[42] The position I defend in this Element, however, is not straightforwardly Carnapian. There are two main differences, which we have seen. Carnap was happy to include more under the heading of *analytic* than I am arguing should be so included here. For Carnap, much that is purely stipulative is included under the heading of *analytic*. The other main difference has to do with the connection between analyticity and tautology. For Carnap analytic truths say are empty or tautological. We saw that this stood in contradistinction to Gödel's view that while mathematical truths are conceptual truths, as they have ontological implications, they cannot be regarded as contentless. The decision between Gödel and Carnap here depends on a definition of content. It is entirely possible that that someone could give a satisfactory definition of *conceptual content*. It also, by the way, seems likely that Carnap would have himself accepted such a definition if it was given in clear terms.

been considering it hopelessly vague? In fact, most concepts we use in every-day life are not only vague but have what Waismann called *open texture* (see Waismann, 1953/1968). Open texture concerns the applicability of the concept to possible rather than actual applications. Take for example the concept of a *blanket*. Blankets tend to be wide and fairly flat. That said, they can also be quite thick, but how thick? We could start with a knitted (square) blanket and then gradually increase the thickness until we are finally left with something that is clearly not a blanket but a woolen cube. At what point did the blanket become too thick for it to be a blanket? This is just one possible way a term like *blanket* is vague. Since we don't encounter borderline cases like these, we don't think of the concept as vague in this way. Most terms of everyday language are open-textured like this; they are vague in ways we have not even considered. Even if they are not typically seen as vague, they are vague with respect to a host of possible but not actual applications.

If the meanings of our everyday concepts are to such a degree vague and open-textured, and analyticity is based on meaning, is analyticity itself then not hopelessly vague? It may be a very difficult matter to say what is analytic of our concept *blanket*. There are presumably all kinds of conceptual truths about any concept. In fact, we might say that even in the earlier example showing the open texture of *blanket*, we expose a constraint on an explication of *blankets*: blankets are never cubes. Even if this is not the most interesting analytic truth, this example shows that while it is not all that easy to identify what is analytic of a concept, it is not impossible. In terms of other everyday terms, it is true, for example, of our conception of weekdays that there are seven days in a week or that Tuesday comes right after Monday. Therefore, much concerning what we ordinarily take to be analytic of ordinary concepts counts as analytic according to the current view.

Of course, the goal of this Element is to defend the view that mathematics is analytic. In the case of mathematics, we can say, with *mathematical precision* what is true of our mathematical concepts. As we saw, Quine says that all of arithmetic is analytic in the sense I am discussing here (although he does not call it that). Or to take another example, it is certainly not a vague matter whether every group contains an identity element. What must be preserved on any explication of the mathematical concept of a group? Well, the axioms of group theory, of course.

I don't really mean to deny that there is any vagueness in what is analytic in mathematics. Some believe that by reflecting on our conception of set, we may identify new axioms which settle the continuum hypothesis. Others might argue for a possible bifurcation of set theory on the basis of our conception of set being somewhat vague. This is not an issue I intend to settle here. To take another example, Quine, we saw, held that any explication of arithmetic must preserve arithmetical laws. But Benacerraf, for instance (Benacerraf, 1965) thinks what I have called the favored contexts, should also include links to our judgments of cardinality and that the less than relation be decidable. Again I will not take a position on these issues. Rather, I just want to point out that the existence of *some debates* on these questions is not evidence that the idea of what is analytic of our concept of number is *hopelessly vague*. In fact this points to the opposite being true. Both Quine and Benacerraf believe it is very clear what any definition of number must satisfy, it is just that Benacerraf takes this to include somewhat more than Quine.

We have seen in this section that everyday language is vague to a much greater extent than mathematics. We have seen as well that there are nonetheless at least some clear cases of analytic truths involving everyday vocabulary. But this will likely suggest to many another problem with *analyticity* as defined here. After presenting his account of stimulus-analytic in Quine (1960), Quine says that this will not play the role traditionally assigned to analyticity as it will include sentences like "there have been black dogs." What is preventing such a sentence from counting as analytic according to the current account? Well, if we look to our best attempts to define *dogs* (or *canis familiaris*) we see that this is defined by reference to these animals occupying a certain position on the phylogenetic tree. For something to be a dog it must have descended from the (now extinct) grey wolf.[43] So if we look at how we characterize the most important concept in "there have been black dogs," we see that this statement does not follow the propositions which characterize the meaning of the concept.[44] But could not some of our concepts be such that the principles we take to characterize them entail some ordinary empirical facts? Of course I cannot rule this out. Perhaps this would show, if discovered, that they would better be characterize in some other way. In any case, the mere *possibility* of such cases does not rule out the present definition as an analysis of analyticity.

The problems discussed in the previous paragraph concern applying the concept of analyticity discussed here to our concepts outside of mathematics. But, again, the main goal of the present work is to show that this concept applies to most of mathematics.[45] There are certain mathematical axioms that are accepted on the basis of what they entail, rather than that they are recognized themselves as being true of our intuitive concepts. Boolos (1971) argues that

---

[43] I do not think the propositions characterizing the concept of dog entail the existence of, for instance, grey wolves, without first assuming the existence of dogs.

[44] I have not discussed the concept *black*, but here again I would maintain that the statement in question does not follow from what we take to be central to this concept.

[45] See Section 2 for how to interpret *most here*.

all of the axioms of Z are true of our iterative conception of set, but the axiom of replacement is not recognized as being true of this concept. It is accepted because it allows us to prove reasonable things and does not allow us to prove unreasonable things. Axioms arrived at inductively like this cannot be said to be analytic in the sense defined in this Element. Most of mathematics is derived from conceptual truths and so analytic in the sense discussed here. If some axioms are chosen for the simplicity they introduce, or because they lead to appealing consequences, then the truths that depend on these axioms are not analytic as here discussed.

5.2 Analyticity and Axiomatics

Some might say that the picture of mathematical truths as analytic discussed in the last section is really not much more than a restatement of the axiomatic method in mathematics. What counts as analytic of the concept of a group, for example, as we saw, is exactly the axioms of group theory and what follows from these. Of course as the axiomatic view is the dominant view of mathematics today, one would not want one's account of analyticity to be in conflict with the axiomatic method. Further, on the interpretation that what I have said amounts to no more than a restatement of the axiomatic method in mathematics, then few if any should disagree with anything I have said. After all, as said, this is the dominant view of mathematics. However, while we identify some axioms by conceptual analysis and then we see what follows from this via axiomatics, not all axioms are arrived at in this way. We saw this in the previous section. Some axioms are accepted on more inductive grounds. These further axioms, and things that are only demonstrable on the basis of them, are not analytic in my sense. So it is not quite true that the view of mathematics I am putting forward here gives us exactly the same picture as the axiomatic view of mathematics.

Still others might contrast the picture of mathematics as following from conceptual analyses to the picture we get from the axiomatic method.[46] In axiomatics we do not care about the intended meaning of the axioms at all, but merely treat them as arbitrarily reinterpretable. Hilbert is famous for saying that concerning the axioms of geometry that for "points, lines and planes" we must always be able to say "tables, chairs and beer mugs." The point being that

---

[46] Patricia Blanchete gave a very interesting talk recently where she compared and contrasted the role of axiomatics and conceptual analysis in the history of mathematics. I would like to thank her for helping me frame certain things clearly.

mathematics abstracts away from the particular meanings of terms and looks only at the logical relations between the terms as stated in the axioms.[47]

But does this abstract character of the axiomatic method imply that conceptual analysis or explication is less important in mathematics? I do not think this follows at all. Take the Peano axioms for instance. Sure when we treat them axiomatically, we can see them as arbitrarily reinterpretable, but the axioms themselves were arrived at via a conceptual analysis. Here we can say much the same thing as Frege did concerning the conception of arithmetic an *aggregative mechanical thought*. Frege emphasizes that it is only possible to operate with figures mechanically once real thought has taken place:

> It is possible, of course, to operate with figures mechanically, just as it is possible to speak like a parrot: but that hardly deserves the name of thought. It only becomes possible at all after the mathematical notation has, as a result of genuine thought, been so developed that it does the thinking for us, so to speak. (Frege, 1884/1980, p. xvi)

Just as we can follow algorithms blindly once they have been developed and proven to work, we can treat a structure completely abstractly once the work of conceptual analysis, to find the axioms which characterize the structure, has been carried out.

5.3 Conclusions

I have put forward an account of analyticity which is immune to the problems which Quine saw with Carnap's attempts to *explicate* analyticity in terms of meaning postulates. Recall that Quine thought Carnap's attempt in terms of meaning postulates was arbitrary and ad hoc in failing to identify what it was about the intuitive concept of analyticity that was to be preserved. This was not part of Carnap's conception of an explication, but it was part of Quine's conception. We used Quine's conception of an explication itself to define a notion of analyticity. The result is an interesting notion of analyticity, which, unlike well-known early twentieth-century accounts, distinguishes between

---

[47] This Hilbertian story traces back to a remark by Hilbert on a lecture by Hermann Weiner and recounted in Blumenthal (1935). In Grattan-Guinness (2011, pp. 208–209) Grattan-Guinness points out that Hilbert is speaking very casually here and must not be interpreted too literally. For instance, what is intuitively true of line and beer mugs is obviously different. Hilbert makes the same point somewhat more carefully in Hilbert's correspondence with Frege. Here Hilbert says that any system of things (Hilbert's example is "Love, Law and Chimneysweep)" which satisfies the axioms under some interpretation also satisfies any theorem (Gabriel et al., 1980, p. 40).

conceptual truths which are analytic and what is merely stipulated and is not analytic.[48]

It was argued that talk of something being made true in virtue of meaning should always be interpreted as *following from principles which characterize the meaning of an expression*. What we take to characterize the meaning of an expression is what is to be preserved in a Quinean explication. As there is nothing particularly epistemic about this concept of analyticity, I looked at Boghossian's arguments in favor of epistemic analyticity and against metaphysical analyticity. I argued that metaphysical analyticity, or something like it, which I would call semantic analyticity, is defensible once the confusion mentioned at the start of this paragraph is cleared up. I then argued that epistemic analyticity is just this same concept, but with certain tentatively held epistemic principles which are used to turn this into an epistemic notion.

In Section 4, I looked at the relationship between this definition of analytic and other notions. For the most part, I argued that the analyticity of certain propositions does not commit one to various philosophical positions associated with earlier views of analyticity. We need not, and should not see analyticity as meaning stipulated truth. A claim's being analytic does not imply that it is empty or contentless. I then argued that whether or not one accepts some form of relativism, with a little pragmatism, there is reason to believe that what is analytic is (fallibly) true. I also explained why I don't see the ontological implications of analytic claims as worrying.

Finally, I argued that while there is a lot of vagueness in ordinary language, which makes it very difficult to determine exactly what is analytic of a concept, this does not extend to mathematics. For mathematical concepts it is usually quite straightforward to identify what must be preserved by any explication of them. I then showed how the view of analyticity fits with the axiomatic method in mathematics. Here I argued that the axiomatic method is useful once the hard work of explication has been carried out.

---

[48] As a referee pointed out, the complement of *analytic* is generally called *synthetic*, but it seems odd to characterize stipulations, for instance concerning "don't-cares" as synthetic. I agree, and would recommend applying synthetic to the complement of both the analytic truths, as defined here, together with the stipulations we accept.

References

Ariew, R., & Garber, D. (1989). *G. W. Leibniz Philosophical Essays*. Hackett.

Barcan, R. C. (1946). A functional calculus of first order based on strict implication. *Journal of Symbolic Logic, 11*(1), 1–16.

Benacerraf, P. (1965). What numbers could not be. *Philosophical Review, 74*, 47–73.

Blumenthal, O. (1935). Lebensgeschichte. In David Hilbert (Ed.) *Gesammelte Aushandlungen*, (pp. 388–429). Berlin: Verlag von Julius Springer.

Boghossian, P. (1996). Analyticity reconsidered. *Noûs, 30*(3), 360–391.

Boghossian, P. (2017). Analyticity. In B. Hale, & C. Wright (Eds.) *A Companion to the Philosophy of Language*, Volume 2, (pp. 578–618). Chichester: Wiley-Blackwell, 2nd ed.

Boghossian, P. A. (2003). Epistemic analyticity: A defense. *Grazer Philosophische Studien, 66*(1), 15–35.

Boolos, G. (1971). The iterative conception of set. *Journal of Philosophy, 68*(8), 215–231.

Bourget, D., & Chalmers, D. J. (2023). Philosophers on philosophy: The 2020 philpapers survey. *Philosophers' Imprint, 23*(11).

Burgess, J. P. (2004). Quine, analyticity and philosophy of mathematics. *Philosophical Quarterly, 54*(214), 38–55.

Carnap, R. (1939/1955). Foundations of logic and mathematics. In O. Neurath, R. Carnap, & C. Morris (Eds.) *International Encyclopaedia of Unified Science* (pp. 139–213). Chicago, IL: University of Chicago Press, combined ed.

Carnap, R. (1945). The two concepts of probability: The problem of probability. *Philosophy and Phenomenological Research, 5*(4), 513–532.

Carnap, R. (1947/1956). *Meaning and Necessity: A Study in Semantics and Modal Logic*. Chicago: University of Chicago Press, 2nd ed.

Carnap, R. (1950a). Empiricism, semantics and ontology. *Revue Internationale de Philosophie, 4*, 20–40. Reprinted in *Meaning and Necessity: A Study in Semantics and Modal Logic*. 2nd ed. Chicago, IL: University of Chicago Press, 1956.

Carnap, R. (1950b). *Logical Foundations of Probability*. Chicago, IL: University of Chicago Press.

Carnap, R. (1963). W. V. Quine on logical truth. In P. A. Schilpp (Ed.) *The Philosophy of Rudolf Carnap*, vol. XI of *Library of Living Philosophers*, (pp. 915–922). La Salle, IL: Open Court.

Chomsky, N. (2000). *New Horizons in the Study of Language and Mind*. New York: Cambridge University Press.

Creath, R. (2007). Quine's challenge to Carnap. In M. Friedman, & R. Creath (Eds.) *The Cambridge Companion to Carnap*, chap. 14, (pp. 316–335). Cambridge: Cambridge University Press.

Ebert, P. A., & Rossberg, M. (2013). *Basic Laws of Arithmetic*. Oxford: Oxford University Press.

Field, H. (1980). *Science without Numbers: A Defence of Nominalism*. Princeton, NJ: Princeton University Press.

Field, H. (1994). Are our logical notions highly indeterminate? In P. A. French, T. E. Uehling, & H. K. Wettstein (Eds.) *Philosophical Naturalism*, vol. XIX of *Midwest Studies in Philosophy*, (pp. 391–429). Notre Dame, IN: University of Notre Dame Press.

Field, H. (1998). Do we have a determinate conception of finiteness and natural number? In M. Schirn (Ed.) *The Philosophy of Mathematics Today*, (pp. 99–130). New York: Oxford.

Frege, G. (1879/1967). Beggriffsscrift: A formula language, modeled on that of arithmetic, of pure thought. In J. V. Heijenoort (Ed.) *From Frege to Gödel* (pp. 11–92). Cambridge, MA: Harvard University Press.

Frege, G. (1884/1980). *The Foundations of Arithmetic*. Evanston, IL: Northwestern University Press, 2nd revised ed.

Frege, G. (1914/1979). Logic in mathematics. In F. K. Hans Hermes, & F. Kambartel (Ed.) *Posthumous Writings*, (pp. 203–250). Oxford: Basil Blackwell.

Frost-Arnold, G. (2013). *Carnap, Tarski, and Quine at Harvard: Conversations on Logic, Mathematics, and Science*. Chicago: Open Court Press.

Gabriel, G., Hermes, H., Kambartel, F., Thiel, C., & Veraart, A. (1980). *Philosophical and Mathematical Correspondence of Gottlob Frege*. Chicago: University of Chicago Press.

Gödel, K. (1995a). Is mathematics syntax of language? (*1953/9-iii). In S. Feferman, J. W. D. Jr., W. Goldfarb, C. Parsons, & R. M. Solovay (Eds.) *Kurt Gödel Collected Volume III Unpublished Essays and Lectures*, (pp. 334–356). New York: Oxford University Press.

Gödel, K. (1995b). Some basic theorems on the foundations of mathematics and their implications (*1951). In S. Feferman, J. W. D. Jr., W. Goldfarb, C. Parsons, & R. M. Solovay (Eds.) *Kurt Gödel Collected Volume III Unpublished Essays and Lectures*, (pp. 304–323). New York: Oxford University Press.

Gödel, K. (1953-9). Is mathematics syntax of language? IV, Unpublished.

Grattan-Guinness, I. (2011). *The Search for Mathematical Roots, 1870–1940: Logics, Set Theories and the Foundations of Mathematics from Cantor Through Russell to Gödel*. Princeton, NJ: Princeton University Press.

Gustafsson, M. (2014). Quine's conception of explication – and why it isn't Carnap's. In G. Harman, & E. Lepore (Eds.) *A Companion to W. V.O. Quine*, (pp. 508–525). Malden: Wiley Blackwell.

Guyer, P., & Wood, A. W. (1998). *Critique of Pure Reason*. Cambridge: Cambridge University Press.

Hofmann, F., & Horvath, J. (2008). In defence of metaphysical analyticity. *Ratio, 21*(3), 300–313.

Kreisel, G. (1967). Informal rigour and completeness proofs. In I. Lakatos (Ed.) *Problems in the Philosophy of Mathematics*, (pp. 138–186). New York: Humanities Press.

Langford, C. H. (1942/1968). The notion of analysis in Moore's philosophy. In P. A. Schilpp (Ed.) *The Philosophy of G. E. Moore*, vol. i, (pp. 321–342). La Salle, IL: Open Court.

Lavers, G. (2008). Carnap, formalism, and informal rigour. *Philosophia Mathematica, 16*(1), 4–24.

Lavers, G. (2009). Benacerraf's dilemma and informal mathematics. *Review of Symbolic Logic, 2*(4), 769–785.

Lavers, G. (2012). On the Quinean-analyticity of mathematical propositions. *Philosophical Studies, 159*(2), 299–319.

Lavers, G. (2015). Carnap, Quine, quantification and ontology. In A. Torza (Ed.) *Quantifiers, Quantifiers, and Quantifiers: Themes in Logic, Metaphysics, and Language*, vol. 373 of *Synthese Library* (pp. 271–99). Dordrecht: Springer.

Lavers, G. (2019a). Hitting a moving target: Gödel, Carnap, and mathematics as logical syntax. *Philosophia Mathematica, 27*(2), 219–243.

Lavers, G. (2019b). Waismann: From wittgenstein's tafelrunde to his writings on analyticity. In D. Makovec, & S. Shapiro (Eds.) *Friedrich Waismann: The Open Texture of Analytic Philosophy*, (pp. 131–158). Cham: Palgrave MacMillan.

Lavers, G. (2021). Quine, new foundations, and the philosophy of set theory by Sean Morris. *Journal of the History of Philosophy, 59*(2), 342–343.

Lavers, G. (2022). Ruth Barcan Marcus's role in the mid-twentieth century debates on analyticity and ontology. In J. Peijnenburg, & S. Verhaegh (Eds.) *Women in the History of Analytic Philosophy*, (pp. 247–272). Cham: Springer.

Leng, M. (2010). *Mathematics & Reality*. Oxford: Oxford University Press.

Morris, S. (2018). *Quine, New Foundations, and the Philosophy of Set Theory.* New York: Cambridge University Press.

Parsons, C. (1995). Quine and Gödel on analyticity. In P. Leonardi, & M. Santambrogio (Eds.) *On Quine: New Essays*, (pp. 297–313). New York: Cambridge University Press.

Putnam, H. (1973). Meaning and reference. *Journal of Philosophy*, *70*(19), 699–711.

Putnam, H. (1975). The meaning of "meaning". *Minnesota Studies in the Philosophy of Science*, *7*, 131–193.

Quine, W. V. (1947). The problem of interpreting modal logic. *Journal of Symbolic Logic*, *12*(2), 43–48.

Quine, W. V. (1995). *From Stimulus to Science.* Cambridge: Harvard University Press.

Quine, W. V. O. (1939/1976). A logistical approach to the ontological problem. In *The Ways of Paradox and Other Essays*, (pp. 107–32). Cambridge MA: Harvard University Press, revised and enlarged edition ed.

Quine, W. V. O. (1940). *Mathematical Logic.* Cambridge, MA: Harvard University Press.

Quine, W. V. O. (1948a). Logic and the reification of universals. *Review of Metaphysics*, *2*, 21–38.

Quine, W. V. O. (1948b). On what there is. *Review of Metaphysics*, *2*, 21–38.

Quine, W. V. O. (1951/1963). Two dogmas of empiricism. In *From a Logical Point of View*, (pp. 20–46). New York: Harper & Row.

Quine, W. V. O. (1951/1976). On Carnap's views on ontology. In *The Ways of Paradox and Other Essays*, (pp. 203–211). Cambridge MA: Harvard University Press, revised and enlarged edition ed.

Quine, W. V. O. (1960). *Word and Object.* Cambridge, MA: MIT Press.

Quine, W. V. O. (1963a). Carnap and logical truth. In P. A. Schilpp (Ed.) *The Philosophy of Rudolf Carnap*, vol. XI of *Library of Living Philosophers*, (pp. 385–406). La Salle, IL: Open Court.

Quine, W. V. O. (1963b). *Set Theory and Its Logic.* Cambridge, MA: Harvard University Press.

Quine, W. V. O. (1969). Ontological relativity. In *Ontological Relativity and other Essays*, (pp. 26–68). New York: Columbia University Press.

Quine, W. V. O. (1976). The ways of paradox. In *The Ways of Paradox and Other Essays*, (pp. 1–18). Cambridge MA: Harvard University Press, revised and enlarged edition ed.

Quine, W. V. O. (1990). *Pursuit of Truth.* Cambridge MA: Harvard University Press.

Quine, W. V. O. (1991). Two dogmas in retrospect. *Canadian Journal of Philosophy*, *21*(3), 265–274.

Quine, W. V. O. (2008). *Confessions of a Confirmed Extensionalist and Other Essays*. Cambridge, MA: Harvard University Press.

Quine, W. V. O., & Carnap, R. (1990). *Dear Carnap, Dear Van: The Quine-Carnap Correspondence*. Berkeley: University of California Press.

Raab, J. (2024). Quine on explication. *Inquiry*, *67*(6), 2043–72.

Russell, B. (1918/1956). The philosophy of logical atomism. In *Logic and Knowledge* (pp. 177–281). New York: The MacMillan.

Russell, G. (2008). *Truth in Virtue of Meaning: A Defence of the Analytic/Synthetic Distinction*. Oxford: Oxford University Press.

Shapiro, S. (1991). *Foundations without Foundationalism*. Oxford: Oxford University Press.

Verhaegh, S. (2018). *Working From within: The Nature and Development of Quine's Naturalism*. New York: Oxford University Press.

Waismann, F. (1949/1968). Analytic — synthetic 1 what is analytic. In R. Harré (Ed.) *How I See Philosophy*, (pp. 122–132). New York: Palgrave Macmillan.

Waismann, F. (1951/1968). Analytic — synthetic 4 contingent and necessary. In R. Harré (Ed.) *How I See Philosophy*, (pp. 156–171). New York: Palgrave Macmillan.

Waismann, F. (1953/1968). Language strata. In R. Harré (Ed.) *How I See Philosophy*, (pp. 91–121). New York: Palgrave Macmillan.

Waismann, F. (1956/1968). How I see philosophy. In R. Harré (Ed.) *How I See Philosophy*, (pp. 1–38). New York: Palgrave Macmillan.

Warren, J. (2020). *Shadows of Syntax: Revitalizing Logical and Mathematical Conventionalism*. New York: Oxford University Press.

Weiner, J. (2020). *Taking Frege at His Word*. Oxford: Oxford University Press.

Wright, C. (2001). Is Hume's principle analytic? *Notre Dame Journal of Formal Logic*, *40*(1), 307–333.

The Philosophy of Mathematics

Penelope Rush
University of Tasmania

From the time Penny Rush completed her thesis in the philosophy of mathematics (2005), she has worked continuously on themes around the realism/anti-realism divide and the nature of mathematics. Her edited collection, *The Metaphysics of Logic* (Cambridge University Press, 2014), and forthcoming essay 'Metaphysical Optimism' (*Philosophy Supplement*), highlight a particular interest in the idea of reality itself and curiosity and respect as important philosophical methodologies.

Stewart Shapiro
The Ohio State University

Stewart Shapiro is the O'Donnell Professor of Philosophy at The Ohio State University, a Distinguished Visiting Professor at the University of Connecticut, and a Professorial Fellow at the University of Oslo. His major works include *Foundations without Foundationalism* (1991), *Philosophy of Mathematics: Structure and Ontology* (1997), *Vagueness in Context* (2006), and *Varieties of Logic* (2014). He has taught courses in logic, philosophy of mathematics, metaphysics, epistemology, philosophy of religion, Jewish philosophy, social and political philosophy, and medical ethics.

About the Series

This Cambridge Elements series provides an extensive overview of the philosophy of mathematics in its many and varied forms. Distinguished authors will provide an up-to-date summary of the results of current research in their fields and give their own take on what they believe are the most significant debates influencing research, drawing original conclusions.

Cambridge Elements $\equiv$

The Philosophy of Mathematics

Printed in the United States
by Baker & Taylor Publisher Services